FOUR TROJAN HORSES OF HUMANISM

Harry Conn

Four Trojan Horses of Humanism

 First published in 1978 and entitled *Four Trojan Horses*.

 Write to Editor, Mott Media, Inc., 1000 East Huron Street, Milford, Michigan 48042.

Robert F. Burkett and Leonard George Goss, Editors

Copyeditors: Leonard G. Goss and Ruth Schenk

Cover design/illustration: A. G. Smith

Typesetting: Professional Composition, Inc.

Printing: House of the Printers

Manufactured in the United States of America

ISBN 0-88062-009-9

Table of Contents

Acknowledgements

I would like to thank the following friends of mine for their assistance and encouragement: Miguel Cruz; Susan Fields; George Otis, III; Michael Cordner; Charles Joseph; Mrs. Pat Manby; Lori Verick; John B. Conlan; and Mrs. Lorraine Fair, my secretary.

Foreword

In each generation there are certain businessmen who are eminently successful in their chosen profession and still have the time, the concern and the genius to understand the crucial issues confronting their generation and to develop practical ways of dealing with those issues.

Such a man is Harry Conn. His years of outstanding leadership in those areas of his personal and deep concern have marked him as a man of intense and very practical ability. In his years of lectureship to fellow engineers he earned their professional esteem while at the same time sharing his personal faith in Christ in a warm and winning way.

With all of his other responsibilities he has had time for diligent study which has prepared him to understand and explain some of the most threatening issues of our time. *Four Trojan Horses of Humanism* has been written by a man who dares to think—to think carefully and long—and who chooses to share his thoughts, insights and opinions with those who dare to think. I urge you to read *Four Trojan Horses of Humanism* at least twice; once to feel the stream of the author's thinking and the second time to follow his close and careful reasoning so as to weigh adequately the force of his arguments.

The author has given me the privilege of sharing this work while it has been in preparation. Because I felt so strongly the need for my generation to share the author's insight into the importance of "incipiency of the will", I urged him to present this in a somewhat more complete manner in an extended appendix. Because he has chosen to do so, I now urge you to give this section of this volume the careful reading it deserves.

—Paris Reidhead

I

Four Trojan Horses of Humanism

Our nation's greatest problem is not one of ecology or pollution. A pine tree produces more hydrocarbons in a day than an automobile. It is estimated by at least one source that ninety-three percent of our pollution comes from nature.[1] Moral pollution is our greatest problem, not physical pollution.

The 1976 Republican National Convention could have been the most important convention in the history of our country, but it turned out to be a colossal flop. The reason it was such a failure was because they didn't face the real issue of our day, humanism. They

[1]Professor John J. McKetta, Dep. of Chemical Engineering, U. of Texas, "The Eight Surprises, Or, Is the World Going to Hell?"

either didn't understand its terrible effect upon our country or they were afraid to face it out of political expediency.

I personally asked one of the two presidential candidates this question: "If you are nominated and elected to office, what are you going to do about stopping the Department of Health, Education and Welfare from propagating their religion of humanism?[2] We are supposed to have separation of church and state." After his ten-minute "answer," a senator standing beside me said, "He didn't like your question, and he didn't understand your question."

I would like to make certain you understand the real issue of our land, which is humanism. Your life can be 100 times more important to our world and our country if you will take the time and trouble to understand what I am going to say.

Not long ago, I was asked to lunch by a very successful liberal arts college president. The purpose of the lunch seemed to be to inform me of the latest trends and developments in higher education. He started by stating that previously our colleges and universities existed for the purpose of training young people to develop a disciplined mind and learn how to study. Then they could lead useful and fulfilled lives, help

[2]Humanism was judged by the Supreme Court as a religion without God. The court ruled in the *Torasco* case (1960) that those who do not believe in God can still have a conscientious objector status on *religious* grounds. The record of the case specifies some non-theistic religions, saying, "Among religions in this country which do not teach what would generally be considered a belief in the existence of God are Buddhism, Taoism, Ethical Culture, *Secular Humanism* and others" (emphasis added).

solve some of the problems of their day and be useful servants to God and their fellowman. He said this is no longer the purpose of higher education. The colleges and universities now exist so that the professors can seek truth in an unrestricted way.

Students are now a necessary evil to pay the freight of the professors' quest. I remarked to the president, "This is quite a paradox, the colleges now exist so the professors can seek something that doesn't exist." With a smile, he agreed.

You are not considered to be educated by some people unless you believe there is no such thing as absolute truth. Even the word *moral* is a dirty word today in most educational circles. This same college president had just returned from a meeting at the University of Wisconsin, which was attended by 400 college and university presidents. They had agreed, but not quite unanimously, that nothing is absolutely right and nothing is absolutely wrong (And they were absolutely sure!). They did, however, agree upon one absolute: belief in absolute, academic freedom. In other words, they'll believe in absolutes when absolutes serve their purposes.

I was reminded of what a friend of mine said to me several years ago and has said many times since. "Harry, the colleges are educating people away from their common sense in many courses." This came from the lips of a man with ten years of higher education.

> Jeremiah 12:5 applies today: "If thou hast run with the footmen, and they have wearied

> thee, then how canst thou contend with horses? and if in the land of peace, wherein thou trustedst, they wearied thee, then how wilt thou do in the swelling of the Jordan?"

Among the many ideas this portion of Scripture conveys is that if the everyday problems of running a business or serving the Lord in a church have made us weary, then how shall we contend or strive with the huge problems of life and those huge problems facing the church and our country?

In the days of Jeremiah, there were two main ways to wage a war. One was on foot and the other on horseback. It was many times more difficult to subdue a warrior on horseback than it was a warrior on foot. For the warrior on horseback had force, power, speed, height and maneuverability on his side, and was a greater tactical problem than a warrior on foot.

The people of God "are running with the footmen," not walking. We are to be diligent in our pursuits, as unto the Lord.

The "footmen" (or problems) in business, for example, might include making an adequate profit, obtaining and training good employees, high accounts receivables, inadequate discounts, increased material and service costs, high sales multipliers, wanting unreasonable discounts, slow mail service, etc.

The "horses" can be symbolic of the huge problems of life. It doesn't mean much to run a successful business if you can't do it to glorify God and serve your fellowman. Additionally, if you don't have religious, political, educational and family freedoms, what does it matter that you can run with the footmen? All of these, we are about to lose, seemingly without a struggle, after many good men gave their lives that we might have them. "How are you going to contend or strive with the 'horses'?"

I am certain that those few in this world who are contending with the "horses" do not go unnoticed or unrewarded by the God of Abraham, Isaac, and Jacob, Maker of heaven and earth, even in this life. Though many may not immediately observe their rewards, they are here nevertheless. As an example: When a servant of our God gives up houses, lands, career, and sometimes his loved ones, he is not concerned for himself. He is, however, vitally concerned (but not worried) about how it will affect his children.

A book was published, *Who's Who of America,* which was a study and analysis of the people listed in *Who's Who*. It was discovered that it took 25,000 laboring families to produce one child that would be listed in *Who's Who*. It required 10,000 families where the father was a skilled craftsman (electrician, tool and die maker, technician) to produce one child that would be listed in *Who's Who*. It showed that it took 5,000 lawyers, 6,000 Baptist preachers, 5,000 Presbyterian preachers to produce one listed in *Who's Who*. It showed 2,500 dentists and only 1,200 Episcopalian preachers or priests to produce a listee. It was found that for every seven Christian missionary families, one of their children would be listed in *Who's Who*. Surely this is a good example of Hebrews 6:10, "For God is not unrighteous to forget your work and labour of love." The person with a right motive of heart, can depend upon the literal fulfillment of Mark 10:29–30 and Hebrews 6:10.

Again, this is not to say that the world or even the church will notice or reward those who "contend with the horses," because in our day we don't stone the prophets, we ignore and ostracize them.

In the following pages I will seek to identify and isolate the "horses" of our day. I will call them the "Four Trojan Horses" and reveal their origin and their effect. I will then go on to explain the "swelling (or thicket) of the Jordan." Every free, democratic society in the world is presently faced with the destructive humanistic powers of the Four Trojan Horses. They are sociological, political, psychological, and theological. Perhaps prior to examination of these Four Trojan Horses, I should refresh your mind briefly on the Greek legend of the Trojan Horse.

The Trojan army kidnapped the Queen of Sparta, Helen, and held her captive in the city of Troy. The Spartans fought an unsuccessful ten-year war with Troy to liberate their Queen. The chief problem the Greeks faced in their quest to conquer the city were the insurmountable gates and walls which surrounded Troy. Ulysses, the Greek hero, thought of the idea of building a huge hollow wooden horse on wheels that could be filled with Greek warriors.

The Spartans made the large horse, deposited it in front of the gate of Troy, told the Trojans it was a gift and seemingly sailed away. The Trojans opened their gates and pulled the wooden horse into the city. A huge crowd, full of curiosity, gathered around the horse. A priest threw a spear against the horse and noticed the hollow sound it made. He said, "This doesn't sound right. Let us investigate this horse in a thorough way before accepting it," but no one paid attention. That night while the Trojans were celebrating, the Greek warriors came out of the horse and opened the gates of the city to the Athenians, who then destroyed Troy.

I am reminded of the time in 1959 just before entering a classroom where I was to lecture at the Massachusetts Institute of Technology. I heard a lecturer say, "The greatest problem we have in the United States is not ignorance; it is believing things and concepts that are not true." These Four Trojan Horses we are about to describe have been responsible for bringing these untruths into popular belief.

I propose to show what has bred these Trojan Horses (the Trojan Horse Farm) and reveal their main areas of activity that are giving off "uncertain sounds" that the churches don't seem able to discern. "If the thinkers of our time cannot catch the imagination of the world to the point of effecting some profound transformation, they must succumb with it."[3]

It is amazing how the average American is unaware of what is going on today and seemingly couldn't care less. This is especially true of corporation officials who are supposed to be good stewards of their

[3]Richard Weaver, *Ideas Have Consequences*, University of Chicago Press, 1976.

stockholders' investment, but support policies and ideologies that destroy the free enterprise system. It is a fact that people do not solve problems of which they are unaware or are unable to define, and this is why I will attempt to scratch some readers where at this time they might not feel an itch!

II

Philosophy —The Trojan Horse Farm

It would appear that we are presently witnessing the dissolution of the West. This dissolution is *political*, indeed, but in even more basic terms it is *moral* deterioration. The reasons are many and will not submit to simple analysis.

All religious, political, psychological and sociological systems are based on philosophical presuppositions, theoretical bases or assumptions. If these presuppositions are false, then all doctrine and ideology based on them will be inconsistent with reality and will produce frustration, confusion and the ultimate disintegration of the society that tries to accommodate them.

We live in a world many consider presently in such a state, and it is my contention that at the root of all this lies a false philosophical presupposition that has become the accepted foundation of our entire social and political order. This false presupposition states that the universe is a closed system of causes and effects and only that which is empirically verifiable is of reality, and all else is meaningless.

At the heart of this false presupposition is the deep split between subjective and objective views of knowledge that came from European philosophers. This has separated the objective level of knowledge, science, from the subjective level of personal knowledge, motives and religion. From this comes the belief that a scientific view of the world can give a complete picture of all that is true, and that man is only a machine, an automaton, that responds automatically to stimuli in deterministic patterns of behavior. *This however is not a scientific conclusion, but a philosophical judgment;* indeed it is truly an affirmation of "faith." This false belief, that science is the sole source of true knowledge, is accepted by the secular world without question, with dogmatic "fundamentalist" certainty.

Philosophy has gone from one extreme to another, from the transcendentalism of the early philosophers to the present-day objectivism. Transcendentalism holds that knowledge of reality is derived only from intuitive sources rather than from objective experience. Objectivism holds that objective experience is the only source of truth. The real source of truth, however, can only come from a combination of these two concepts.

"Subjective" and "objective" are not opposites, as is now widely held, but are conjunctive. The words "subjective" and "bias" are *not synonyms,* as present-day objectivism would have us believe.

Immanual Kant, with his formula of "Critical Philosophy," structured the whole philosophical foundation that characterizes all precise thinking about the world; in the philosophical, scientific, historical and religious fields. Kant built and systematized his philosophy on the thinking of the mid-17th century French philosopher, Rene Descartes. Such philosophy is founded, built and developed on the basis of the subject/object distinction. The phrase and formula used to change the pattern of most philosophical thinking was "I think, therefore I am."

With the development of the experimental method of objective science, a new kind of certainty became possible in science. Any knowledge that could not be tested or verified by the methods of objective science was scorned. Such knowledge was not considered wise and cultured. Thus, to speak of a revealed knowledge of God and His acts was to speak nonsense. Man was essentially a mind who simply thought about the objective world. Science became the ultimate and only source of true knowledge. Anything that could not be investigated by the empirical method of science was not considered real.

That which could not be tested through the scientific method was relegated to the sphere of feeling, the subjective. It was never a problem of ontology (dealing with the nature of reality). Rather, it was a problem of epistemology (dealing with the nature of knowledge). Knowledge that could not be verified scientifically was at first thought simply subjective. Then this subjective knowledge became questionable. Finally, it was denied to be knowledge at all!

Thinking had been split into two levels: the objective level for science with its empirically attested facts, and the subjective level for religion and such other emotionally confirmed convictions. This basic secular presupposition established that whatever "cannot be examined and tested by the methods of empirical science is not in the deepest sense 'real' and cannot become an object of knowledge or a source of truth."[1]

As humans we use both eyes together to see things in four dimensions, including time as a dimension. If we were to use only one eye, our view would be three dimensional and therefore flat. Imagine how distorted life and surroundings would be if we only used one eye to view them. In a natural sense this is tantamount to the philosophical claim that the empirical scientific method is the only source of knowledge and truth. It is a distortion!

Incidentally, what distortions have been born from this subject/object distinction? This split between the objective and the subjective was initially the birth cradle of *existentialism*. Strangely enough, though, existentialism (which accepts as the final court of truth

[1]Robert J. Blaike, *Secular Christianity and the God Who Acts*, Grand Rapids, Mich., William B. Eerdmans Publishing Company, pp. 38–39.

man's own self) arose as a reaction against the exclusive claims made by empirical science. Kierkegaard vehemently protested against science's claim of having the sole source of truth. Thus, for the existentialist there was no absolute truth. There was no universal right and wrong. Every man became his own law. This became truth to the existentialist.

The split between the subjective/objective was also the birth cradle of *pragmatism*. Truth became based on social change. Science claimed that unless knowledge could be tested or verified through its empirical methods, it was not truth. Thus, to be able to deal with man with any sort of meaning, the experience itself became truth, since morality and the like could not be proven scientifically.

Pantheism eventually took root as well. Since God could not be proven scientifically, He was merged with nature. The world itself became divine. Thus, God became essentially a part or aspect of the objective cosmos. This way, God could be retained with the subject/object split.

The genesis of *amorality* emerged from the subject/object distinction. Law and morality certainly could not be tested or verified empirically. Therefore, morals ceased to exist, and the resultant amorality was predictable.

There is no place for personal freedom, or freedom of the will in this objective view of truth. Therefore, this objective view affirms the universal determinism of natural causes and effects. Everything is caused and determined in the universe.

This subject/object split placed man basically as a thinking subject with the world as the object of this thinking. Thus, man is not an agent free and able to act in the observable world. Man cannot make purposeful or intentional changes in his world. He is simply responding to the stimuli of his environment. This is the very foundation of B. F. Skinner's behavioral psychology. Man is a product of his environment and his heredity and nothing else. There are no choices or decisions. Wiped out is any form of accountability, responsibility or freedom.

M. Polanyi,* a distinguished physical chemist, wrote a monumental work on scientific method entitled *Personal Knowledge*. He states that "scientific severity, with its strict empiricism, threatens the position of science itself. The intellectual passion for achieving absolutely impersonal knowledge results in massive modern absurdity."[2] This absurdity has almost entirely dominated twentieth century thinking on science. Empirically speaking, persons cannot be recognized, therefore science presents a picture of the universe in which man himself is absent!

*Polanyi says that knowledge exists only in the human mind (no man, no knowledge). Words on paper aren't knowledge, they are paper and ink marks that stand for knowledge. Extremists (pseudohumanists) seek to purify knowledge by totally depersonalizing it. Hence, to succeed, they must remove man entirely. But if they do that, then they wind up with no knowledge.

[2]M. Polanyi, *Personal Knowledge* (University of Chicago Press), p. 9.

IF IT IS TRUE, IT CANNOT BE TRUE!

According to the objective level, the empirical methods of science are the sole and adequate source of all knowledge and criterion of reality. Yet, *man as observed* by the scientist is a machine, an automaton. This is so because rational intentions and purpose are unscientific; therefore, they do not exist. This reduces man to a computer, a machine. Man is conditioned or determined by the causal events of his environment and past. However, the same must be true of *man as the observer* of the observing scientist. Thus, when the scientist sets forth a proposition or a theory of truth based on the scientific method, it is not really due to the scientific method. He was rather compelled to put it forward. It was determined; it was caused. There was no deliberate act in affirmation of the truth by the scientific method. In addition, the theory being presented will be accepted or rejected by the hearers in the same way. Not that evidence through scientific method has convinced anyone. The stimuli that existed at that moment caused them to reject or accept, whether it was true or not, whether it was scientific or not. Thus, truth itself as a meaningful concept is voided. If truth is to be meaningful, it must mean that a theory was affirmed as true, as opposed to another one.

Truth and its discovery must involve choice. Yet the very essence of the scientific method, of the empirical objective method of science, disallows the recognition of the existence of choices: *If it is true*—if it was a concept selected over another by decision—*it cannot be true,* because the scientific method doesn't recognize the existence of decision. In other words, man is subjective as the observed subject and/or the observer scientist. If the objective, empirical method is to be carried out to its logical conclusions, truth as truth cannot exist because subjectivity, which is unscientific, is always present. Absolutely impersonal knowledge is unable to recognize any persons. Absolutely impersonal knowledge presents us with a universe in which we ourselves are absent, and so is God.

As Blaike says, "In such a universe, there is no one capable of creating and upholding scientific values; hence, there is no science. We find at the end of such an inquiry that man dominates a world in which he himself does not exist."[3] "The inevitable conclusion, logically, from the premise of Descartes, is that the universe is a mere machine and that 'God is dead'."[4]

Abortion, euthanasia, genetic engineering, social engineering, the existence of an elite class of men: these are the logical consequences that result from such a presupposition. In the view of this philosophy, which is the basis of most modern fields today, man has no more meaning than a mere rock.

Francis Schaeffer traces this problem back to Hegel's dialetic and the abandoning of the antithesis/thesis thinking. Though this might be true to a large degree, it really is not the root of the problem.

[3]*Secular Christianity and the God Who Acts,* p. 178.
[4]Ibid., pp. 23–24.

Schaeffer doesn't go back far enough. The subject/object distinction lies right at the heart of the problem. We must reject entirely this subject/object distinction.

Scientific knowledge is essentially and properly objective; but it only comprises a part, an important and specialized, yet biased part, of our total knowledge. It is still a "one-eyed view." There are other non-scientific sources that account for our nonscientific knowledge. We need the two-eyed view, the phenomenal and the noumenal. The noumenal is knowledge reached by intellectual intuition without the aid of the senses, a thing in itself above and beyond the grasp of science. Descartes' formula, "I think, therefore I am," only recognizes phenomenon. Therefore, by itself, it is distorted and invalid. We must keep the subject/object together; we must have the phenomenal and the noumenal. His formula should have been, "I act, therefore I am." An act is not a mere event; an act is originated by intention, by purposeful thought; it recognizes the existence of man and of God. This must be the base of man's thinking if he is to achieve integrity. Otherwise man is doomed to absurdity.

SUMMARY:

If the premise, "The universe is a closed system of causes and effects," is accepted, and is followed with "only that which is empirically verifiable is of reality and all else is meaningless," then the very concept of the dualism between subjective/objective is only a structural convenience used to pigeon-hole those phenomena whose causal antecedents are beyond our current technological ability to detect. Every feeling, intention, decision, and emotion of every subject arises from adequate causes which could not be opposed.

Therefore, the very reaction against this deterministic position by men such as the theologian Bultmann must be determined or caused, as are any positions held and defended by any man, including the objective scientist. If this premise of a totally closed system is true, then the scientist who is throwing his influence on the bandwagon of empiricism is himself not *choosing* the best system. He is responding to stimuli he has no power to resist.

Although empiricism is defended in virtually every discipline, in this extreme of causality, it is the antithesis of the practical programs that currently make up our economic, political, law enforcement, social and recreational agencies. In high schools, students have gained more freedom of choice in their curriculum. In the apprehension and investigation of lawbreakers, motives are considered, as are past offenses. Politicians strive to persuade us that they share our concerns so that we might choose them on election day. Advertising agencies try to produce the best ad campaigns, and the jobs, salaries and benefits of their agents depend on their success. Yet in a closed, causal system, everyone is equally successful at being what the impersonal successions of causes has made them. No one could possibly break out of the mold. The deification of empiricism seems to be equivalent to the concept that "whatever is, is right." This is nonsense! I readily admit that the everyday common sense person does not hold fast the intellectual perplexities contained in the subject/object split, but it is rarely the everyday common sense person who is making the policies and programs by which we must live and worship and raise our children. Really, a person shouldn't be very old before he knows the words "objective" and "scientific" are not synonyms.

It is not my intention to imply that all scientists believe in the subjective/objective split. In fact, many scientists are not so enamored with scientific analysis as are the more "popular" scientists.

III

Psychology —Trojan Horse

The very term "mental disease" is nonsensical, a semantic mistake. The two words cannot go together except metaphorically; you can no more have a "mental disease" than you can have a purple idea or a wise space. A "mental disease" is said to be a "disease" of the mind. A "Mind" is not a thing and so technically it cannot have a disease. "Mind" is shorthand for the activity and function of the brain. It is thinking, remembering, perceiving, wishing, imagining, reasoning and all the other activities of which the brain is capable.[1]

According to the National Institute of Education over 52,000 junior and senior high school teachers in the United States are the victims of brutal assault by

[1] E. Fuller Torrey, M.D., *The Death of Psychiatry*, Penguin Books, Inc. New York.

their students. In the United States, students are allowed to physically assault their teachers because there is no code of conduct. At the same time, the teachers are not allowed to spank their students. In the city of Chicago, it is common knowledge that it is more dangerous to be a public school teacher than it is to be a city police officer.

REASON WHY

A few years ago, one of our U.S. Supreme Court Justices made this statement in an address: "When a man kills his wife and four children, we should not blame him for what he has done but look into what caused him to do it."

When you understand the many fallacies of this almost unbelievable statement, you are on your way to understanding the Freudian Trojan Horse. I acknowledge that most psychologists have departed from many of Freud's original postulations (although most were not original with him and even the old Freud was not the same as the young Freud), nevertheless, his basic premises are still with a great majority of professional and drugstore phsychologists. These revisionist positions seek to destroy the religious meaning of guilt. They attempt to dissolve religion by rendering guilt a medical or a biological problem. In other words, they make crime a sickness instead of sin, holding forth the unintelligent notion that all people are in some sense sick mentally. Even non-Freudians mouth that phrase, having picked it up by osmosis rather than thought. Freud made sex a purely biological function and removed it from the realm of morality; the result: not even homosexuality is considered immoral. The whole Freudian theory is based upon the Lamarkian theory in evolution, yet there is probably not a physical scientist in the free world that believes that species pass on through heredity the necessary acquired characteristics.

Almost simplistically stated, the Bible teaches that God governs or rules over four distinct realms[2] They are the inanimate realm, animate or animal realm, providential government and the government of free moral action. God governs or regulates in the inanimate realm (sun, moon, stars and anything made up of the 92 or more chemical elements and the ten or more synthetic elements) by the law of cause and effect. He produces a causation and he gets the desired effect every time. There are probabilities in man's cause and effect, but not with God. This is physical government which follows God's physical laws (Psalm 119:91–92). There are hundreds of examples in Scripture of God's providential government which are abnormal or unusual in coercing man's will to cause man to do certain things which will fulfill God's eternal purposes (e.g., Ezra 1:1; John 11:49–51). When God *causes* a man to do something, he gets no reward or condemnation because no free choice was involved and it did not stem from any right or wrong intention of heart. Providential

[2]Gordon Olson, *The Moral Government of God,* Men for Missions, P.O. Box 6109, Minneapolis, Minnesota 55406.

government is not referring to man's salvation, because in salvation God never tinkers with man's will (Acts 26:19).

We can accurately state that what is caused cannot be free. Nor can that which is caused be accountable or responsible. The Bible contains over 2000 verses indicating that man is born with a free will despite what B. F. Skinner concludes. A man can commit an act so many times that it becomes a habit. This habit eventually becomes his nature, and man is bound by the chains of his nature. Jesus came to break every fetter, but God holds man responsible for the antecedent choices that formed the habits and nature. There is only one verse in the whole Bible that some would claim to show it is possible to "cause someone to sin," but it is in the infinitive mood which has a *may* or *may not* (see Matthew 5:32). Jesus wants to forgive man, to set him free to live a life of righteousness and partake of the divine nature.

It can also be said that what is free cannot be caused. That which is free is accountable and responsible for its choices, choices which are either praiseworthy or blame-worthy. When a person really understands the true nature of sin, one giant light goes on in the human soul. Man can be influenced to sin, but cannot be caused to sin. An influence is not an irresistable force whereas a causation cannot be resisted. A person can have reasons for sin, but not any cause.

B. F. Skinner's "advances" in science may be found in the writing of Robert Owen (1771–1858), whose major work, *A New Society, or Essay on Principle of the Formation of the Human Character,* expounds the theory that man's character is wholly determined by environment. Behaviorism wasn't true in the 18th century and it still isn't true.

INCIPIENCY OF THE WILL

In the 19th century, enlightened Christians had a phrase, incipiency of the will, a concept that this century desperately needs to learn for its survival and influence. Man is created in the image of God, and among other essentials of this image is a free will. The "incipiency of the will" means that man has the mysterious ability to originate his own actions apart from any outside or inside influence. He can say yes or no to a good influence and can resist or yield to a bad influence. This is a noumenal concept as opposed to phenomenon. It goes beyond the borders of science which stop when an act, material, intention or event cannot be touched, tasted, smelled, seen, heard or put in a test tube.

In Mark 6:6 speaking of the town of Nazareth, it says Jesus marvelled at their unbelief. I think if gestures were recorded, it would say Jesus scratched His head. Look at the sociology of this situation. Jesus, the only begotten Son of the Father, lived sinlessly in their town. I think He had the same heredity, with the exception of conception, as His half brothers and sisters, or He could not have been tempted in all points like as we are, yet without sin (Hebrews 4:15). Yet, they were offended at Him and did not believe on Him (though some did after the resurrection). So look at the environment, heredity and truth they had, and yet they said no to this good influence.

The text says Jesus marvelled at their unbelief. He didn't diagnose or psychoanalyze their unbelief. He knew that as the Savior and sin bearer, He could be a good influence and a good teacher, but He could not cause good or right conduct. He could not cause His hearers to accept or reject Him. He marvelled at the evidence and truth they resisted and rejected. They undoubtedly had *reasons* (although invalid) for rejecting Christ, but certainly no *causations*.

We live in a Freudian age; accordingly, when a person does something wrong or is guilty of some aberration or crime, we ask, "What caused it?" Inherent in this question is an attempt to relieve the guilty of free will, accountability, responsibility. Unfortunately . . . it will not relieve them of their guilt.

I live in a city where a few years ago a fine, 15-year-old boy, named Joey Didier, disappeared one morning while on his paper route at 5:30 a.m. He was never seen alive again. About three weeks later, he was found hanging by the neck in a cottage of a Boy Scout Camp about 70 miles away. He had been abused to death by a homosexual sodomite truck driver. After much diligent police work, the culprit was arrested and he confessed. He obtained a change of venue from our Circuit Court to the Circuit Court of Rock Island, Illinois, for trial. During the trial, it was revealed he had abducted and sexually molested another 10-year-old boy about ten years before in a small town about 50 miles from our town. He had been convicted and given a very long sentence. He was turned loose after six years because the prison doctor said, "We thought he was cured." By saying this, the doctor made him out to be "sick" instead of sinful, mean, degenerate, irresponsible and guilty of a heinous crime.

According to sociologists, man is a product of society. This social determinism, with its categories of *behaviorism, functionalism,* and *voluntarism,* makes society responsible for everything man does. Individual responsibility has been abandoned in favor of social responsibility. The inevitable conclusion of this teaching is that society must be responsible for crime and deviancy, since it is responsible for all man's social behavior.[3] Personal blame and guilt then lose their traditionally accepted meanings; after all, you can't really "blame" someone for wrong action that was not the result of a personal choice, but was the inevitable consequence of his past history. Man, then, can't help what he is doing. He is a helpless victim of heredity and social factors. He is bound to do whatever he does. If you can't really "blame" someone, then it's not right to punish him either, so it is not at all surprising, to find present-day sociologists calling for the elimination of our prisons and jails. These demands

[3]David Lyon, *Christians & Sociology,* InterVarsity Press, pp. 52–53. I do not mean to convey the idea that some instances of chemical imbalance, syphilis, tumors, etc., cannot be the cause of mental problems or aberrations. But these are a minute minority.

are logical and consistent if social determinism is true and social responsibility is allowed to replace individual responsibility. However, these presuppositions, according to the Bible and our own personal experience, are wrong.

The Bible is the only book of truly "preventative psychology" ever written. The church needs to learn the difference between a weakness and a disease. You cannot reason with a sickness; try to educate or talk a person out of a case of smallpox. If mental problems are a sickness, then why talk about them at $70 an hour to a psychiatrist?

A disease by definition is an abnormal condition of an organism, especially as a consequence of infection or malfunction, that impairs normal physiological function. The word physical doesn't mean mental, so how could a mind, which is an activity, be sick or have a disease? Counseling won't change a disease or sickness but it certainly can help a weakness. And to be quite frank, mental disease is a contradiction in terms and mental problems are problems in living, not diseases. If the brain does get a disease, what is needed is not counseling but the help of a neurosurgeon. Diseases have causative agents or physical deficiencies or malfunctions. Weaknesses have influences, lack of strength lack of knowledge, lack of desire to face reality and fulfill responsibilities.

A person with a weakness can be strengthened to cope with stress through truth, love, exercise and concern, and God's church should have these in great supply. Why do our preachers and teachers lay down and play dead for the "Freudians" when even Freud said he only offered an understanding of the problems, not any solutions? Christian workers must wake up.[4] The greatest evangelist our country has ever had, in my opinion, was Charles G. Finney. He said it was the Christian worker's job to take sides with God against sin and tear down all of the sinner's hiding places.

The Bible teaches that sin is not natural to man (Romans 1:29-31; II Tim. 3:13), and is willfully committed. "Triumphs" against the natural order of living exact unforeseen payments. Man was created for the throb of holiness, not for the supreme gratification of self, and when man sins he is violating his design and can only reap the painful consequences of his unintelligent choices. This explains why there is no peace for the wicked. We need to teach people that when they choose a course of action, they are also choosing the consequences that are inseparably connected with the act, regardless of whether it is a good act or a sinful act. Those consequences may last a lifetime and into eternity (Galatians 6:7).

William Glasser, in his book *Reality Therapy*, says his mental patients are not "sick," they are crazy." The reason he calls them crazy is because they are committing crazy acts. The reason they are committing "crazy" acts is because they are not getting their basic needs fulfilled. (This exludes those... mental problems

[4]The following titles provide excellent reading on the subject: *The Myth of Mental Illness* (Szasz), *The Crisis of Religion* (Mowrer), *Integrity Therapy* (Drakeford), *Freud* (Rushdoony).

that stem from a chemical imbalance or malfunctioning of some organ.)

Glasser says man has two basic needs: to love and to be loved. It isn't any wonder that God commanded us to love one another, because when we do, we fulfill a need in our brother's life and a need in our own life. He created man with a need for love to properly function, just as man designs an automobile to run on gas to fulfill the purpose for which it was designed. His three R's of Reality, Responsibility and Right need to be taught to the whole world, because we reap (as consequences of our choices and acts) what we sow.

> But what of those who deny that mankind is the standard, and who hold that biblical faith requires separation and division? The prophets of mental health of this religion of humanity know the answer: they are mentally sick. God's hell is outlawed, but a new hell has opened up to apostates: mental sickness, with its many mansions. Mental health is so defined that not only political and economic conservatives but all orthodox Christians are clearly sick. Did not Freud say that religious people avoided the personal neuroses by accepting the cosmic neurosis? The fact that they are more responsible, stable and neurosis-free is itself proof of their sickness, i.e., acceptance of the cosmis neurosis, God! The prophets of mental health must be given free reign to 'heal' mankind by a 'vast

reorganization of the world.' The results of the mental health programs have been a steady encrouchment on civil liberties of a most flagrant sort. The power of the psychiatrist is the foundation of a new and more fearful inquisition. The relationship of the psychiatrist to courts of law is increasingly seen by many as 'threat to society.' To criticize the mental health movement is to draw fire on oneself as mentally disturbed and also, an added 'evil', a champion of political and economic conservation. [5]

Dr. Stanton E. Samenow has worked at a federally-run, Washington mental hospital and has learned that criminal behavior is not a mental illness and cannot be reversed by giving people education, jobs or money. Samenow said the experience caused the psychologists there to throw out beliefs that people committed crime because they felt guilty and subconsciously needed to be punished. Samenow said he and his colleague Dr. Yochelson identified 53 separate thinking patterns that each of their 225 hard-core criminals, from white-collar crooks to grade school dropouts, had in common. Those characteristics included anger, pride, sentimentality, lying, intolerance of fear and procrastination. While many people have

[5]Rushdoony, *Freud*, Presbyterian Reformed Publ. Co., Nutley, N.J., pp. 64, 65.

some of these qualities, he said criminals "have them all at an extreme."

Yochelson found that his subjects, about half of whom had been admitted to St. Elizabeth's hospital after being declared insane, weren't insane at all. Samenow said he and Yochelson sought to change thinking patterns of the criminals that had developed over a lifetime, and in recent years experienced considerable success. Certainly this provides convincing evidence that mental problems and crime stem from moral problems. Perhaps some day we will follow the Apostle Paul's method to show people that they are guilty instead of pathetic.

Glasser says the conventional weakness of psychology and psychiatry has been that we have left out morality. In a 1974 issue of *Psychology Today* magazine, he stated, "When you go to a therapist, all you are doing is buying a friend." Commenting further, Dr. Glasser remarked, "You could get rid of all of us psychologists and psychiatrists and the world would never miss us."

In his book, *The Death of Psychiatry*, Dr. Torrey forcefully proves the fallacy of calling mental problems a disease. He defines them as problems in living. He says only 5 percent of the people in mental institutions are there because of physical problems of the brain such as brain tumor, syphilis, and so on, and they should be treated by neurologists, not by psychologists and psychiatrists. In private practice the percentage is much less. Torrey writes:

> In a society permeated with the ideals of democracy and the Judeo-Christian faith, we have been wary of trying to solve social problems . . . for all the impersonal elements in them . . . in ways that ignore the fact that most social problems are rooted in the personal choices that individuals make daily. In brief, the personal ethic has been regarded as the substratum of the social ethic.

The only place in the universe where man can get his guilt truly resolved is at Calvary (Hebrews 9:14). Why throw our fellowman into the Freudian coliseum when we have a Savior in Jesus Christ, the church and the Christian family to supply the love all people need, and the "balm in Gilead" to solve the guilt problem?

If you have been around college campuses and other places of inquiry, it isn't uncommon to hear such a remark, "If there is a God why doesn't He do something about all of the suffering in the world?" When one understands that Christ died not only so the guilt penalty could be transferred from the guilty to the innocent, but also to reduce the amount of suffering in the universe, it is very apparent that God is vitally interested in reducing and eliminating suffering.

While I am grateful for every Christian and secular hospital in the world, and every humanitarian agency working to alleviate physical and mental pain, when the atonement of Christ on Calvary is fully understood it can be seen that Jesus Christ is doing more than all of the combined human agencies of man to alleviate suffering. He is doing this by forgiving and transforming people so that they can lead a benevolent life and so terminate the infliction of pain and suffering upon others and themselves by their own selfish misconduct. This is not to deny or denigrate the divine physical healing taking place every day.

Therefore, Jesus Christ, God's only begotten Son, died not only to release man from the power and penalty of sin, but also to alleviate and eliminate pain and suffering. What more could He have done ?

Dr. Edward Pinckney, in his book *The Fallacy of Freud and Psychoanalysis,* writes:

> But even though there has been questioning of the Freudian system, the rules of that system remain such that it cannot be subject to a real scientific inquiry. Right from its start, and with no obvious changes today, the concepts of psychoanalysis have been interpreted as immutable principles rather than hypotheses to be tested and discarded if found faulty. There is not one single "scientific" experiment on record to support the doctrine that psychoanalysis . . . as defined by Freud as a form of treatment for mental illness . . . has, or can, cure anybody or any illness! In constrast, there is a wealth of documented information to show that the results of psychoanalysis are not only

unsuccessful, but what is even worse, have been harmful.

Again, I feel the answer lies in the assumption or rejection of responsibility. If you are willing to assume your share, you will conquer every conceivable obstacle to good mental health. If, on the other hand, you spend your efforts trying to dodge moral obligations, you cannot help but bog down in your own mire of self-created doubt . . . which leads to worry, which leads to anxiety and which finally leads to your seeking help for something you will not do for yourself.

So it is that little more than fifty years ago, one solitary sick man . . . a man who could not stand to have people look at him; a man who had abnormal feelings about his own mother at the expense of his wife; a man who vicariously reveled in sordid sexual stories . . . brought forth a doctrine to justify and excuse his own abnormalities.

Psychoanalysis is attractive to those who wish to be relieved of responsibility for their actions and failures. This seems to document very well the fact that psychoanalysis does more harm than good.

And all I hope to do is to burst the bubble of belief in psychoanalysis and, by so doing, reverse the tide that has saturated our culture and permeated our everyday activities. To me, psychoanalysis is a hoax . . . the biggest hoax ever played on humanity. By showing who analysts are, how they work, what they believe, and what they have done, I hope to show Freud as a fraud. If I succeed, I am idealistic enough to hope that the world may return to the belief in love, ideals, good taste and courtesy . . . and the "books" that have been burned by the Freudian Inquisition.[6]

[6]Edward Pinckney, M.D., *The Fallacy of Freud and Psychoanalysis*, Prentice-Hall, Englewood Cliffs, N.J.

IV

Sociology —Trojan Horse

The most common philosophical mistake of our day is to confuse secular humanism or any other kind of humanism, be it "scientific," "ethical," "democratic" or "religious," with the type humanism once propounded by Erasmus. Humanism should never be equated in our day with humaneness. Humanism is the most inhumane philosophy ever concocted on our Lord's green earth. It is now the religion of sociology. Humanism is man (autonomous man) starting with man to build himself a world view and a philosophy of life that eliminates God and any divine dimension.

Karl E. Keefer, in his book, *Facing Today's Problems*, defines humanism in this manner:

> Humanism is the belief that man has within himself sufficient resources to solve his problems without help from a supernatural Power or Person. Secularism is the outgrowth of this belief and regards religion as outmoded superstition or incorporates it into the rest of life. The sacred and secular become indistinguishable, not because all things are sanctified by the will of God, but because all things, even the most sacred, are secularized by the will of man.

Secular humanism is the summation of all that is anti-God. Communism is humanism with a political disguise. The nature of humanism is that the ultimate end of all human striving is the happiness of man. Sociology never seems to have learned that man never finds happiness by seeking it; it is only achieved by serving one's fellowman and by voluntarily losing one's life for Christ's sake in service to Him.

We have turned our country over to the "white coats," the psychologist, psychiatrist and bureaucrat in Washington to make decisions and policies that govern the country in which we live and raise our children. The humanistic "white coats" do not often believe in the concept of biblical morality and therefore have no sound theoretical foundation, such as the Ten Commandments, upon which to base their theories.

If one has no sound moral basis on which to order life, there will be no intellectual perplexities, let alone pangs of guilty conscience, over the following humanistic innovations:

1) Legalized abortions
2) Euthanasia (mercy killing)
3) Genetic engineering
4) Birth control (The state will decide who procreates)
5) Housing (take our children on Monday morning and get them back Friday night)
6) Acceptance of homosexuality
7) Acceptance of suicide

The Humanist Manifestos I and II[1] were drafted in 1933 and 1973 respectively, and signed by leading humanists such as John Dewey, B. F. Skinner and Sir Julian Huxley. These two documents define the philosophy that has been reshaping our society, and is now the foundation of public education in the United States. Following are some excerpts from these documents.

> We find insufficient evidence for belief in the existence of a supernatural; it is either meaningless or irrelevant to the question of the survival and fulfillment of the human race. As non-theists, we begin with humans, not God; nature, not deity.

> We affirm that moral values derive their source from human experience. Ethics is autonomous and situational, needing no theological or ideological sanction.

[1]See the Appendix.

> We deplore the division of humankind on nationalistic grounds. We have reached the turning point in human history where the best option is to transcend the limits of national sovereignty and to move toward the building of a world community in which all sections of the human family can participate. Thus we look to the development of a system of world law and world order based upon transnational government.

I would like to quote extensively from the paper "Religion of Humanism in Public Schools," to offer some background on how our schools are propagating this false religion:

> I often think about the religion of Humanism being promoted in public schools and without fail, I find myself asking, Where, oh WHERE are the Christians? Why do those who claim to be true followers of Christ permit this hoax to go unchallenged? Every Christian and every Christian church should be actively exposing and working to remove this Godless religion from our public schools. One woman's efforts resulted in a ban on prayer and Bible reading. How is it that the people of a nation that claims to be predominately Christian cannot rout the religion of Humanism from their schools? The reasons are many, but I think the main reason that Christians are not working harder to rid pub-

lic schools, and often, their own church schools, of the menace of Humanism is that they simply don't know what is meant by the word "Humanism," or they are not sure just how the religion of Humanism manifests itself in the schools.

So today, I am going to try to achieve an understanding of Humanism as it exists in the schools so that you will know what to look for when you are examining your child's books and materials.

Before we do anything else, let's clear up what we mean by Humanism or Humanistic education. These days we hear the word "human" and other "human" sounding words used to describe what's going on in the educational process. We hear of the need to teach children to be "humane" and we think it means children are being taught to be kind and compassionate with each other. We hear that schools are promoting "human understanding" and improved "human relations." To the average person, unskilled in the deceitful semantics of educationese, such "human" sounding words convey the idea that education is a civilizing process, and this is where we lose many parents.

Unless specifically defined otherwise, the terms "humanistic education" or "humanism in the schools" or "educating for humaneness" or "educating for human understanding" or whatever, all mean the same thing: The promotion of the principles of the religion of Humanism.

Quite often some know-it-all, would-be intellectual will approach me, and looking disdainfully down his nose with overbearing patience, will inform me that I'm WOEFULLY confused . . . that Humanistic education means teaching what is known as the humanities . . . the great classics. But that's not the case . . . and I have proof, straight from the horse's mouth, so to speak, from none other than the program officer for the National Endowment for the Humanities, William Russell. Writing in the August 1975 issue of the Journal of Education of Boston University's School of Education, he offered his description of Humanistic education which included the following. He said, "An initial clarification to make is that the term 'humanistic' is not the adjectival form of the noun 'humanities.' Humanistic education does not mean education in the humanities disciplines."

So let us nevermore be confused about the definition of Humanistic education. It means promotion of the principles of Humanism.

The next thing that must be done is to obtain a copy of the Humanist Manifesto I and II. I used the second Manifesto because that's what the Humanists are currently working from most diligently. I can't stress too strongly that it is absolutely vital that you recognize and understand the major articles of faith expressed in the Manifesto for it is these principles or articles of faith that are being inculcated in your children. Remember, Humanism as promoted in the schools is not some nebulous, intangible thing that we know is there but cannot touch . . . it is very real and can be identified very easily once you know what you are looking for.

Specifically, what are some of the principles or articles of faith of Humanist belief that find their way into public and even private education? Above all, Humanists do not believe in God and, of course, they do not believe in salvation or damnation. They believe in the theory of evolution, a theory that is often presented as fact in many schools and textbooks. Humanists believe that everyone has a right to full sexual freedom, the right to express their individual sexual preferences as they desire. They believe that everyone, regardless of age or condition has a right to determine the values and goals that affect their lives. They believe in the right to suicide, abortion and euthanasia. They adhere to situation ethics morality, meaning they do not live by or believe in absolute standards of morality. They recognize no immutable rights or wrongs as revealed in the Ten Commandments. They believe everyone has a right to maximum individual autonomy, meaning the right of each to do his own thing, whatever it may be. Humanists do not believe in national sovereignty, but in a world government.

These are the major articles of faith or principles of Humanism as outlined in the second Humanist Manifesto. How are they applied in public education? Very simply. Every course in the curriculum can serve as a vehicle to promote Humanist beliefs . . . history, math, literature, languages, social studies, sex education, environmental education, home economics . . . everything. Over the years during the steady influx of Humanist influence in the schools via the use of Humanist-oriented textbooks and teachers unknowingly trained to become missionaries of Humanist beliefs, over many years . . . Humanist influence has been steady and subtle. However, we have reached a point where apparently it has been determined our society and schools are ready for intensive indoctrination into Humanism because we now openly have the ultimate apparatus for promoting Humanism in the schools and it's called "values education."

When you bring up the subject of values education, someone will always insist that teachers have always been involved in value information, and indeed this is so. It is impossible for a teacher to avoid conveying values to students. Her voice, her dress, her general demeanor, all convey values of some sort. However, in years past, the values conveyed by teachers in the main, reflected parental values, or at least, reflected those values that were considered in accord with prevailing Judeo-Christian morality. In years past, there usually wasn't a value conflict between schools and parents.

However, today we have a whole new ball game. Young teachers coming out of teachers colleges have had a thoroughly Humanistic education. Many of them, in the process, have lost the religious faith of their youth, or, they hang on to their religious orientation in name only or adopt some ersatz Christianity. They are quite ready to promote a system of values that is at odds with the traditional Judeo-Christian ethic. They are quite ready to facilitate a value system that will promote Humanist beliefs, and in fact, that will create practicing Humanists. Many young teachers, thoroughly indoctrinated into Humanism have a missionary zeal that would put so-called Christians to shame.

Now, about values education. Let's look at the rationale for having values education in the schools at all. What is the justification offered by promoters of values education? The best answer can be found in a book titled, "Values Education: A Handbook of Practical Strategies for Teachers and Students," written by the three most prominent leaders in the values education movement . . . Sidney B. Simon, Leland W. Howe and Howard Kirchenbaum. The authors explain that young people brought up by moralizing adults are not prepared to make their own choices about what they want to believe.

They ask, and I quote, "How does the young person choose his own course of action from among the many models and many moralizing lectures with which he has been bombarded? Where does he learn whether or not he wants to stick to the old moral and ethical standards or try new ones?"

Well, where he learns whether or not he wants to stick to the old moral or try new ones is in Humanistic values education. And this book gives the teacher 79 different ways to help the student discard the values he has come to school with, and find new ones. And lest you still doubt the intent of values education, you should read a book titled

"New Principles in the Curriculum," by Louise M. Bernam. She states very clearly that it is a proper role for the schools to change, create and clarify student's values.

Now, let's see how values education is used to promote those Humanist beliefs.

A series of papers published by the Adirondack Mt. Humanistic Education Center, Upper Jay, New York, explains most compellingly how values education promotes Humanist beliefs.

Let's start with sex education. In one of those papers titled, "Sexuality and the School," by Marianne and Sidney Simon, the authors tell us that too many teachers are not merely asexual, they are downright anti-sexual, to the degree that they cause sexual destruction in the schools by causing children, as they put it, to wrinkle up like raisins in the sun. The Simons boldly declare, "Some changes are desperately needed. Schools can no longer be permitted to carry out such a horrendously effective program for drying up students' sense of their sexual identity. The schools must not be allowed to continue fostering the immorality of morality. An entirely different set of values must be nourished."

And this is precisely what is happening in sex education. If you still naively think sex education deals only with the facts, be aware that sex education goes beyond the mere teaching of physiology and biology. Sex education openly and frankly deals with development of attitudes and values. The fact that sex education often extends from kindergarten through grade 12 should tell you that more than teaching the facts of sex is going on. Anything a child needs to know about sex at any given stage of his development can be explained to him in a very brief period of time by you, a clergyman or physician. It doesn't take 12 continuous years, unless of course, you are trying to establish or alter values, attitudes and behaviors along with the facts.

The presumption of sex education is that children come to school without values or with values that cause them to wrinkle up like raisins in the sun . . . values that must be changed. A goal of sex education is to eliminate harmful myths and hangups, that are, according to Humanist belief, and here I quote from the Manifesto, "fostered by intolerant attitudes, often cultivated by orthodox religions and puritanical cultures . . ." Such "repressive" attitudes about sex prevent children from attaining their full potential as "sexual beings" and prevent them from expressing, according to Humanist terminology, "their sexual proclivities and (to) pursue their lifestyle as they desire." And you've seen the product of this permissive Humanistic philosophy . . . young people with a scorn for Christian standards of morality, open homosexuality, rampant VD and untold numbers of abortions.

For children from a home where strong traditional moral values and standards of behavior are stressed, conflict and guilt are likely to ensue if they choose to depart from their moral upbringing. They have been taught about salvation and damnation which they can't easily dismiss. So what is the solution? One way to get rid of the Christian "myth" of salvation and damnation is to teach death education. Interestingly, many death education courses are taught by sex educators, which is quite logical. Sex education tells students sex is for fun, and this is followed by death education, which in accord with Humanist belief, teaches that this life is all there is . . . There is nothing after death. So, if Humanistic sex and death education are effective, young people can pursue their sexual proclivities as they desire, in keeping with Humanist teaching, because they have been taught in death education that heaven is here and now, and they will not have to worry about salvation or damnation because this life is all there is.

Another Humanist principle, the belief in situation ethics morality, finds its way into just about everything, but let's take drug education for example. Information is presented to students from the position that "we are giving you all the facts . . . you make up your own mind as to how you will use the information." Children without wisdom or maturity are given loaded information and told to make up their own minds about how they will use the information! Then need we wonder, when under peer pressure or under the influence of drug-oriented rock music and "entertainers," whom they idolize, that they decide to use drugs? Christians believe that the body is the temple of the Holy Spirit and is not to be abused. Humanist philosophy says make up your mind . . . what's important is having fun here and now, for this life is all there is. Lives shattered by disease and addiction are the monuments to Humanistic situation ethics behavior, fostered by Humanistic, situation ethics values education.

Another Humanist principle is the belief in the right of maximum individual autonomy . . . the right to do one's own thing, whatever it may be. A dictionary defines "autonomous" as meaning "without outside control." Some time ago in the county in which I live there was an uproar over a questionnaire administered in the schools by Johns Hopkins University. Parents were outraged by the many questions that invaded student and family privacy. Parents were justified in their outrage, but they completely overlooked the purpose behind the questionnaire, which was to determine how autonomous the students were becoming! A report issued by Johns Hopkins explained that one of the goals of "open education" which is a euphemism for Humanistic education . . . was to develop self-reliance and autonomous behavior. The report stated, "A major part of the growing up process is developing a willingness to act autonomously, to no longer have to depend on one's family or others for excessive guidance and decision-making help . . ." Common sense tells us that we cannot take immature children, lacking wisdom and turn them loose to act autonomously with any degree of responsibility. This was recognized by education Thomas B. Gregory, in an article in the November 1971 issue of "Educational Leadership." He warned that in becoming autonomous, "Internal controls may not develop, and seeking autonomy may become the immature action of simply resisting further external control. As a result, seeking autonomy may include experimenting with asocial actions (delinquency)."[2]

There were 646 church related colleges in the United States in 1846 and not 10 non-church related colleges of importance. The Land Grant Act, signed by President Lincoln in 1862, gave us the state-supported colleges and universities, and it is very evident where they obtained their teachers. Needless to say, it was the church's influence in education that produced the following kind of thinking:

> People need a way of acting justly, both as individuals and as groups. A person, to maintain his integrity and probably his sanity, needs some consistent idea that his acts will produce certain results, including rewards or punishments. A society, to survive intact, must have some system to decide between right and wrong, and balance out its rewards and punishments.[3]

It was taught that a man's heredity, environment and training will determine his destiny, and that man doesn't have any choice in this destiny. Dr. Viktor Frankl disputes this set of factors and says the main factor has been left out, that of choices.

[2]Barbara Morris, *The Religion of Humanism in Public Schools*, P.O. Box 412, Ellicott City, Maryland 21043, 1976.

[3]Stanley J. Rowland, Jr., *Ethics, Crime and Redemption*, Philadelphia, The Westminster Press, p. 76.

One of the most thrilling truths of Christianity is this: Whatever deficiencies we may have had in our heredity, environment and training, if we will choose to turn from our selfish ways, seek and find the Lord in true conversion, we will get a new Father who will help and love us. The Spirit of God will dwell in us (which is a welcome change in our inner environment) and teach us His ways. We then have the power to change our environment for good and become a part of the solution to the world's problems.

SECULAR HUMANISM AMENDMENT

The amendment to the Higher Education Act Amendments of 1976 (H.R. 12851), called the Conlan Amendment after the Honorable John B. Conlan, was passed by the House, but defeated and eliminated in the Senate.[4]

The bill stated:

> No grant, contract or support is authorized under the Foreign Studies and Language Development portions of Title II of the bill for any educational program, curriculum research and development, administrator-teacher orientation or any project involving one or more students or teacher-administrators involving any aspect of the religion of Secular Humanism.

Many bills have been before Congress which I personally think are intended to bring about the systematic destruction of Christian influence and its institutions. One example is the Youth Camp Safety Act (HR 6761). This would impose health and safety standards on all youth camps (over and above those already imposed on camps by some six Federal agencies, and up to twelve State agencies). Government standards would also be set for camp directors. In

[4]See Onalee McGraw, *Secular Humanism and the Schools,* The Heritage Foundation, Washington, D.C.

North Carolina alone it is estimated that 75 percent of the youth camps, many of them Christian camps, would have inadequate funds to meet these new additional Federal standards.

Another example is the Charity Disclosure Bill (HR 41), which would have the effect of repressing charitable giving. Another example was the proposed Genocide Treaty, which the Carter administration urged the Senate to ratify. This treaty would have subjected American citizens to the jurisdiction of an international court for the alleged crime of causing physical or mental harm to a single member of any specified ethnic, racial or religious group. Americans would have no constitutional protection of their rights, as treaties become "the supreme law of the land," and can override present constitutional guarantees. The treaty excluded political genocide, as it would allow governments to liquidate any particular group by classifying them as "enemies of the state." However, the crime of "causing mental harm" is covered by the treaty, and this can mean any *attempt* to change the cultural, religious or social mores of any group. On this basis, Protestant and Catholic missionaries could be charged with "genocide." This treaty could have possibly caused the return home of every foreign missionary and be the lawful end of obedience to the Great Commission.

When I think of sociology and its god, secular humanism, I am reminded of this axiom: It has been observed by sages throughout the ages that man's calloused heartlessness toward his fellowman increases in proportion to his unconcern about God.[5] What good is it to have the assurance of material and physical welfare without love, joy, peace, longsuffering, gentleness, goodness, faith, meekness, temperance or self-control? (Galatians 5:22–23)

The euphemism "humanism" is clever: the word itself is a Trojan Horse beguiling people ignorant of its true definition. It is unwise and confusing to interchangeably use the words cause, a physical term, with influence and reason for behavior, and expect any accountability and responsibility for conduct. Slums may be an occasion of crime, but never a cause. Influence is only a moral antecedent and cause is that which inevitably brings an effect and is always an amoral event.

[5]See Miceli, *The Gods of Atheism*, Arlington House, New Rochelle, New York, p. 115.

V

Politics —Trojan Horse

If science is the only source of truth (which is the natural outcome of the subject/object split), then everything except the material must be excluded. Thus, scientific materialism becomes god and man is a mere machine controlled by the principles of cause and effect. In this philosophy man is seen as the product of society, and problems in human behavior are seen as social problems which can only be solved by controlling and changing the society which produced them. Socialism, then, is the logical and consistent political ideology of humanism and materialism. We define socialism as the centralized control of society wherein the individual is considered incapable of making the choices necessary to order his own life. These decisions are made for him by the elitist ruling class who supposedly know what is best, and man becomes the servant or tool of the state. Thus, it is believed, social problems can be controlled out of existence.

Let us consider for a moment how successful the socialist ideology has been in solving the problems and providing the needs of society. Since the last century, we have seen the rise of a militant form of socialism called Marxism, which has produced the state of Soviet Russia. Russia has a population of some 230 million people, and with its collectivist farming system needs 39 million farmers, plus large food imports from other countries to supply its needs. By contrast, the United States, with a population of 220 million people, needs only 3.5 million farmers to supply all the nation's food requirements, as well as to produce large food exports to many other nations (including Russia). In fact, were it not for a form of free enterprise within Russia wherein the farmers are allowed to keep and sell for themselves what they can grow in the corners of the fields and in their backyards, Russian farming output would be far less. A comparison of the industrial output of these two nations tells the same story. In fact, but for frequent massive grain supplements to Russia since 1917, and American technology (acknowledged by Stalin as making Soviet heavy industry possible), Soviet Russia would have long ago collapsed.

That the free enterprise economic system produces far more than a state controlled economic system is beyond any reasonable doubt. Furthermore, the wealth that a free economy produces benefits everyone in that society. (If anyone doubts this, they should compare the general living standards, the availability of material goods and services, and the extent of personal freedom in Russia and the United States.) As this country continues what some consider its headlong rush towards socialism, it is surely a most perplexing matter to consider why a free people, with such a good system of production as we have in the U.S., would want to trade it for the statist or collectivist system of Russia. There citizens are unable to feed themselves and have no personal freedom or right to worship.

We shall now consider how the political policies of humanism have affected the stability and even the very existence of our great nation. Liberalism, and the attendant socialization of the U.S., has led to the point where our survival as a free, sovereign nation is gravely threatened. The ideological struggle between communism and the free enterprise system that has dominated world politics for the better part of this century is fast approaching a showdown. One side must ultimately win and swallow the other; many feel they cannot continue in coexistence. There has been a steady decline of American influence and power throughout the world in the face of growing communist might. Our foreign and domestic policies that have led to this point are puzzling and fraught with inconsistencies to the average, thinking, patriotic American. However, once we understand the presuppositions and ultimate objectives behind our policies, then our recent history and present position are very understandable, clear and consistent.

What are these presuppositions that have guided American policy since World War II?

Firstly: Communism is changeable; the Soviets now want peaceful coexistence.

Secondly: Nuclear war is unthinkable; we must have peace at any price.

Let us examine briefly the validity of these presuppositions. Communism cannot change without being inconsistent with itself. Its avowed aim *is* and *has* always been the "liberation" of the working masses of the world from "imperialistic capitalism", and the ultimate victory of communism over the entire world. Lenin, Stalin, Khrushchev and Brezhnev have all affirmed this. Their *methods* have changed, but *not* their goals.

"Peace" to the communist mind means the absence of any opposition or threat to communism. It is their basic and unchangeable doctrine that there can be no peace until communism controls the world. Detente is not an alternative to war, but an essential preparation for it. It is a means to an end, to be discarded when no longer useful. The Soviet history of broken treaties and agreements affirms this philosophy.

Furthermore, the Soviets do *not* believe nuclear war is unthinkable. In fact, they believe it is both survivable and winnable.[1] It is perhaps untrue that nuclear war would end all mankind, and that our

[1]Maj. General George Keegan, "New Assessment Put on Soviet Threat," Aviation Week & Space Technology, March 28, 1977, p. 40; Richard Pipes, "Why the Soviet Union Thinks It Could Fight and Win a Nuclear War," Commentary, July, 1977, p. 34.

nuclear weapons are sufficient to "overkill" the entire Russian population.[2] It has been estimated by defense analysts that in an all-out nuclear war with Russia, with their civil defense system there would be 10 million casualties.[3] This is less than Russian losses in World War II. Furthermore, publications and information from Russia show they have come to a similar conclusion.

If our political leaders believe that we must have peace at any price, then they will sacrifice anything for peace—even our freedom. However, if history tells us anything, it tells us this—nations under bondage do not, and cannot, live in peace. The oppression of increasing state control has always ultimately produced those who are willing to fight and die in order to throw off their oppressors and regain their freedom. This is the history behind the settlement and founding of this great nation.

It is evident then that these presuppositions we have just examined are very questionable. However, they continue to be the basis of our foreign policy. The purpose of this policy has been to allow the Russians to catch up with us and go on to a position of military superiority. In fact, President Reagan has become the first chief executive in our nation's history to claim that the Soviets are actually militarily superior to the U.S.

[2]Richard E. Pipes, "Nuclear Weapons Policy Questions," Aviation Week & Space Technology, November 6, 1978.

[3]Eugene Kozicharow, "Nuclear Attack Survival Aspects Studied," Aviation Week & Space Technology, November 14, 1977; Joanne S. Gailar & Eugene P. Wigner, "Civil Defense in the U.S.," Foresight, May-June, 1974; T. K. Jones, M. R. Edwards, "Deterrence and Civil Defense," ACU Education and Research Institute.

From this position, some liberals claim the Russians are supposed to feel more "secure" and, therefore, less likely to launch a preemptive strike against the U.S. This would, therefore, mean greater security to the U.S. (Note how fatally dependent this concept is on the presupposition that Soviet communists would be satisfied with peaceful coexistence.) The essence of this philosophy is effectively summarized by Harvard Professor Richard E. Pipes, who is the former Director of the Russian Research Center at Harvard (1968–1973). In an article for *Commentary,* he says the central doctrines of the disarmament lobby have been that "An American monopoly on nuclear weapons would be inherently destabilizing." Professor Pipes continues, that "to feel secure, the United States actually required the Soviet Union to have the capacity to destroy it . . . Modern strategy . . . involved preventing wars, rather than winning them, securing sufficiency in decisive weapons rather than superiority, and even insuring that potential enemy's ability to strike back." These propositions, under the name of "Mutual Assured Destruction" (MAD), have been the core and essence of American foreign policy since the early 1960s.

This policy explains at least to some conservatives why this country has spent over one trillion dollars on defense since 1967 without adding one single nuclear ballistic missile or one single heavy bomber to our strategic forces. This also explains why the explosive power of our total strategic missile force has actually decreased by a factor of some 10 since 1962. Over this same period of time, the Russians have added many hundreds of nuclear ballistic missiles to their strategic forces.[4]

If we look at the overall strategic balance, as of 1977, Russia had some 3,500 strategic offensive weapons compared to our 2,100.[5] The imbalance of nuclear power is actually far greater than these figures would indicate due to the much larger size of the Russian missiles, the total payload weight of their missile fleet being some five times greater than ours. Also, these figures ignore the intercontinental ballistic missile (ICBM) refire capability of the Soviet Union. They employ a "cold launch" technique which makes it possible to immediately reuse many of their ICBM launch silos after initial use. The U.S. ICBM silos do not have this capability. Commenting on this, recently retired Chief of Air Force Intelligence, Major General George Keegan, has said:

> My suggestion is that today the Soviets have somewhere between 500 and 3,000 additional ICBMs that can be refired which are totally ignored in discussions of the strategic balance . . .[6]

[4]Annual DOD Report, FY 1977: John M. Collins, "American and Soviet Military Trends," The Center for Strategic and International Studies, Georgetown University.

[5]Annual DOD Report, FY 1977: "The Military Balance," 1975–1976, International Institute for Strategic Studies.

[6]"New Assessment Put on Soviet Threat," op. cit., p. 46.

It must also be remembered that more than 50 percent of the firepower of our nuclear force is carried by bombers,[7] consisting almost entirely of an aging and obsolete force of some 300 B-52 bombers. In an attack on Russia, these subsonic aircraft (designed in the 1950s) would have to face some 2,700 interceptor aircraft and over 12,000 surface-to-air missiles,[8] coordinated by a vast interconnected radar network, which according to General Bruce Holloway, former Commander of the U.S. Strategic Air Command, consists of some "25 times as many radars as the United States." Our ability to penetrate these defenses with even a small percentage of our B-52 force is being increasingly questioned. If we therefore simply consider the comparative strength of the U.S. and Russian missile forces, we see that the Russians have over seven times the explosive firepower that we have.[9] These figures would suggest an overwhelming nuclear superiority.

In conjunction with their greater offensive capability, the Russians have also undertaken a massive civil defense program. Major General George Keegan has reported that, over the last 20 years, the Soviet Union has literally gone underground. Their essential military, industrial and communication installations have been removed from our ability to destroy these

[7]"Pentagon's Inside Size-Up of U.S. Military Power," U.S. News and World Report, January 17, 1977.

[8]"American and Soviety Military Trends," op. cit.

[9]Ibid.

blast-hardened underground installations which now exist in the tens of thousands. They are the hardest man-made structures in the world. It appears also that their entire industrial population are now 100 percent protected by vast underground bunker systems.[10] China has also constructed a similar program. The Russian and Chinese civil defense systems are said to be better than 90 percent effective against nuclear attack. As a result, American losses in an all-out nuclear war would be many million more than Russian or Chinese losses.[11] While Russia and China might survive such losses, emerging as still viable, powerful nations, we would probably not.

In addition to their civil defense program, as we have seen, Russia also has a vast strategic defense system of interceptor aircraft and radar guided surface-to-air missiles. By contrast, the United States has one-tenth the number of interceptors and no effective surface-to-air missile system.[12] Also, if General Keegan and his former intelligence staff are correct, the Russians could be close to developing a charged-particle beam weapon, bringing to reality the proverbial death-ray.[13] According to General Keegan, this country

[10]"New Assessment Put on Soviet Threat," op. cit., p. 42.

[11]The U.S. Joint Chiefs of Staff have admitted that in a nuclear exchange, U.S. fatalities would be some 10 times higher than Soviet fatalities. General Keegan is of the opinion they could be 35–40 times higher.

[12]Annual DOD Report, FY 1977 by then Secretary of Defense Donald Rumsfeld.

[13]"Soviets Push for Beam Weapon," Aviation Week & Space Technology, May 2, 1977, pp. 16–23.

is 20 years behind the Soviets in this field.[14]

It can be seen that the Russians are in a greatly superior strategic offensive and defensive position, and this gap widens as Soviet military spending continues to accelerate. Although the SALT[15] agreements allow for considerable Soviet military growth while effectively freezing our own position, the clear evidence is that they are violating the agreement, and increasing their commanding lead far beyond the agreement.[16]

Under a SALT II Agreement, Soviet supremacy would have been even furthered. This was recognized by the Committee on the Present Danger, a private group formed to educate the public on national defense issues, including such men as Dean Rusk, former Secretary of State; Paul Nitze and David Packard, both former Deputy Secretaries of Defense; Admiral Elmo Zumwalt, Jr., former Chief of Naval Operations; and Eugene V. Rastow, former Under Secretary of State for Political Affairs. In a report from this group, authorized by Paul Nitze, it is stated:

> From the beginning of SALT at Helsinki in 1969, the Soviet objective has been to

[14]"New Assessment Put on Soviet Threat," op. cit.

[15](Strategic Arms Limitation Talks).

[16]Admiral Elmo Zumwalt, "Zumwalt Disputes Policy on SALT," Aviation Week & Space Technology, Jan. 19, 1976, pp. 46–50; "SALT Violations Confirmed," Editorial, Aviation Week & Space Technology, Dec. 12, 1977; Melvin Laird, former Secy. of Defense, writing in Reader's Digest, Dec., 1977.

preserve the U.S.S.R.'s gains and momentum, while encouraging maximum restraint upon U.S. programs. In the classic Soviet Fashion, negotiations have been regarded as a means of stalling and impeding the adversary's momentum while maintaining its own.[17]

Democrat Paul Nitze is also a former senior member of the U.S. SALT negotiating team (1969–1974). He stated in a Washington news conference in November, 1977 that under the present Administration's SALT position, the Soviets would gain an "overwhelming" nuclear advantage which would lock this country into a position of nuclear inferiority. This warning has also been given by Dr. Igor Glagolev, former advisor to the Soviet SALT team who defected to the United States in 1976. He maintains that the SALT II treaty under consideration "does not diminish Soviet superiority in the aggregate power of strategic weapons. The treaty would perpetuate this superiority."[18] (Note that Dr. Glagolev reflects Soviet realization of their *present* strategic superiority over the U.S.)

If all the Russians want is peaceful coexistence, we may well ask why don't they slow down and channel their resources into solving their critical domestic problems? Why do they continue their massive buildup of *both* nuclear and conventional

[17]Reported in "U.S. News and World Report," July 18, 1977.

[18]Reported in "Human Events," December 28, 1978.

forces? The only answer that can logically explain their policies and actions is that our official defense policy presuppositions are totally wrong, and the Russians are, in fact seeking world domination. They fully intend to "bury the west" as they proclaim.

Our nation continues to consistently pursue the policies that have produced the present situation. Assuming then that our leaders *want* peace and are not trying to precipitate war, we can draw the following conclusions:

Firstly, our leaders do not intend to bring about world peace from a position of American military strength and superiority. They have seemingly eliminated our former superiority.

Secondly, our leaders cannot intend to insure world peace by living in peaceful coexistence with a balance of U.S./Soviet military power. The Russians are obviously not cooperating.

Thirdly, our leaders must then be intending to insure world peace by some other ends which have not been officially proclaimed.

Fourthly, these other ends must transcend party politics, because the means are pursued with consistency no matter who is in power.

Fifthly, the only end or objective that logically fits all the evidence, in my own personal perspective, is the ultimate integration of the Soviet Union and the United States into a world federation with a one-world government.

The biggest stumbling block to the establishment of this world federation is a military and morally strong

United States. What we are witnessing in this country is actually the systematic destruction of our military might and our moral fiber from within to open up the path for world federation. The foreign and domestic policies of this nation have for some time been completely and exclusively consistent with this objective. This should not be surprising, since it is a major goal of humanists.[19] Many of our policy makers are humanists, utterly dedicated to their cause.

Many citizens and political commentators are becoming increasingly concerned over the state of our nation and believe we must try and awaken our political leaders to our seriously weak defense posture and to the policies that are destroying personal freedom and the private economy. It does not seem to occur to these people that our leaders might know exactly what they are doing and where they are leading us. Our national destiny is, in fact, being determined and pursued without the consultation or consent of the people or even the Democratic or Republican Parties. This country which started out as a Republic is no longer even a democracy. We are virtually an oligarchy.

The end of the course we are presently pursuing is a worldwide totalitarian state in which personal freedom and incentive is completely suppressed. Conformity to the dictate and ideology of the state is mandatory in order to maintain the humanistic idea of "peace." History has known many cruel dictatorships in the past, when the will of a ruling person or group has

[19]Humanist Manifesto II; See the Appendix.

controlled the actions of people. However, never before has such a state tried to control the minds of its people. This absolute form of control has only become possible with the advent of modern technology and psychological persuasion, with their methods of mass communication, indoctrination, surveillance, monitoring and control. This final totalitarian state to which our policymakers are leading us, will be the most absolute, the most brutal, and the most oppressive this world has ever seen. We are in the throes of the greatest conflict of history—the battle for the minds of men. It is being waged now, in the media, in our schools, our churches, our council chambers, our legislative bodies and in our policymaking board rooms; and freedom is losing. Humanism, with its concepts of worldwide political "peace," through the control of man and society, is winning.

Does anyone care?

For a thorough convincing that the above is no wild-eyed assessment, you should read some of the books on "Community Psychiatry" which masquerade as preventive psychology such as those written by Gerald Caplan, Lindeman, Frantz Fanon Duhl, L. K. Frank and Robert Coles. They have programs and have government money in many instances to carry them out. Their books show how the psychiatrists are becoming more active in politics and what lies in store for the Christian or anyone else who disagrees with them.

VI

Theology —Trojan Horse

Humanism, Secular Christianity, Christian Atheism, Holy Worldliness, and such other self-contradictory terms, express well the confusion of modern theology. The past errors of Marcion, Arius, Pelagius, and others — who were judged by the church to lead followers away from Christian truth — are all minor compared with the fast, compounded error of the separation of the subjective realm from the objective realm.

The theology that results from such a presupposition sets forth a gospel in which "there is no miracle, no resurrection of the body, and no belief in a life after death." God's part with nature or history is ruled out altogether. God becomes futile and useless and quickly ends up as a dead God. Such thought, which is the base of today's religion, philosophy, history and science, finds its origin in an obsolete conception of the universe, derived from the 18th and 19th centuries. It holds that our universe is a closed mechanical system. All things are, therefore, explained naturalistically through the unbreakable chains of cause and effect. The consequence of this thinking gave rise to an abstract, impersonal and mechanistic view of the world.

Men who have made more than a superficial study of revivals know that we are the third or fourth consecutive generation of Christians that have not seen revival. It is true that there have been a few little snatches of it here and there, but not in the sense our nation experienced under a Charles G. Finney. We must have a supernatural visitation of the blessed Holy Spirit in the realm of theology that will have a profound effect upon the sociological, political and psychological realms. If not, this nation of ours is doomed to a "one-world" assimilation.

This assimilation will be the death knell to the "preaching of the gospel" and will usher in a "one-world religion." It will also usher in Matthew 24:9. (It doesn't have to happen in our generation.)

If the Christian is truly evangelical, in the sense that he believes God deserves our determined, persistent efforts to tear down the sinner's hiding places, then he will challenge the objectivity of any discipline, philosophy or world view which relegates the activity of the Savior to the realm of "meaningless" subjective experience. We must affirm the personal experience of salvation as wholly personal and unique (because each of us is unique). At the same time, we must insist that the facts of salvation in history and in its public aspects are objective and verifiable, and that the fact of salvation in the individual life is verifiable by the objective change in the character and works of the saved.

The subjective/objective dualism relegating spiritual matters to the subjective realm has allowed for easy believism, because a person can now have a subjective experience of salvation apart from any objective change in his life or any grasping of the objective truths of Christ.

Feelings of shame, remorse, contrition, the need of forgiveness and "relative peace," may all be experienced in the Christian meeting because the Holy Spirit is working to convert a sinner. This may be misinterpreted to mean the *presence* of the Holy Spirit is a salvation *relationship* when the gospel is stripped of the call for objective holiness of character and works meet for repentance in external relationships with others.

> Much has been written today, particularly among psychiatrists like Carl Jung, Viktor Frankl and Ira Progoff, to the effect that there are laws inherent in the very structure of man to disobey which is to court loss of

integrity, i.e., literal disintegration and insanity.[1]

The church in our day has no conception or understanding as to what God meant when He asked, "Then how wilt thou do in the swelling of the Jordan" (Jeremiah 12:5)? Crossing over Jordan is not symbolic of dying and going to heaven, but of possessing the heritage of the "promised land" which ushered the Israelites into real spiritual and even physical warfare. It is symbolic of a time of great trial, testing, challenge and faith in possessing their inheritance and their souls. Two and one half tribes wanted to stay out of the fight and remain in the fine grazing land east of Jordan. They were admonished, "Be sure your sins will find you out" (Numbers 32:23). It seems like most Christians in our day think II Timothy 2:3–4 doesn't apply to them, but I am certain it does, together with Numbers 32:23. The Jordan was out of its banks and they didn't have a rowboat or drawbridge to their name to enable them to cross the Jordan. It took a real life of obedience and faith. The "swelling of the Jordan" seems to me to be symbolic of times and conditions that will usher in II Thessalonians 2:3 and Matthew 24:9. It is a matter of historical and spiritual fact that when God gives people a supernatural job to perform, if they will do the possible, He will do the impossible.

To "cross over the Jordan," we are going to have to realize that the Lord did not give us the Bible to get

[1]Robert B. McLaren & Homer D. McLaren, *All to the Good*, The World Publishing Co., New York & Cleveland, p. 145.

mankind to agree to go to heaven. The purpose of the Bible is to reveal a great, wonderful and lovable God; and that man is separated from this God and needs to be reconciled[2] to God and his fellowmen. The Bible supplies the truth that the Holy Spirit uses as the means to draw men to Christ (John 6:44–45). The Scriptures were given for doctrine (teaching), for reproof, for correction and for instruction in righteousness.

Humanism has thoroughly invaded evangelical doctrine and is producing libertines. Jesus doesn't invite men to "come and live," but to "come and die." If you die, you shall live. Whittaker Chambers in his book, *Witness,*[3] makes the following comment, "For I cannot hate even an enemy, as I said in a broadcast immediately after Hiss's second trial, who shares with me the conviction that life is not worth living for which a man is not prepared to die at any moment."

Men are admonished to "accept Jesus" so they can go to heaven when they die. The real motive for preaching ought to embrace the fact that Jesus deserves the due reward for His suffering . . . "those for whom He died" (all the people of the world). We don't seem to be aware of what "sin" does and has done to God and that He deserves to be obeyed. We seem preoccupied with what sin has done to man.

God said to Israel, "I am broken with your whorish heart." Yet the Scriptures teach that a man

[2](To reconcile means to cause one thing to cease and another to take its place, to be restored to favor, to adjust our differences.)

[3]Henry Regnery Co., Chicago, Illinois, 1952.

reconciled to God through Jesus Christ can, by virtue of the indwelling presence of the Holy Spirit, live a life that will bring joy to the heart of God, who will rejoice over man with joy and singing.[4] All sin is a transgression of God's law and is unintelligent, harmful, unnatural, selfish, illogical, unphilosophical and must be repented of. Why? Just to get to heaven? No! It is because of what it does to ourselves, our fellowmen and to God.

True Christianity is not an imposition into a life of selfishness, but a whole new life in Christ. We don't give Jesus our time, our time *is* His. Humanism says the ultimate end of all being is the happiness of man. Christianity teaches that the ultimate end of all being is to glorify God (render Him excellent by our conduct and manner of life) and to love our fellowman as we love ourselves. *A theology that depersonalizes God, dehumanizes man.* At the heart of the crisis of our times lies the cold belief of millions that the death of religious faith is seen in nothing so much as in the fact that "it has lost its power to move anyone to die for it."[5]

However, true Christianity *is* worth dying for; but this will not be perceived until it has been purged of cheap grace, easy believism and humanistic motives.

C. G. Finney taught and proved that when truth is preached with an anointing of the Holy Spirit with a suitable amount of prayer and a life of devotion to back it up, revival is assured.

[4]Zephaniah 3:17–18.
[5]Whittaker Chambers, op. cit., p. 700.

MORAL LAW

The secret to the great conviction of sin, as characterized by the great revivals held by Finney, was his attitude toward the moral law or Ten Commandments. If we ever have revival again, this will have to be rediscovered and preached.

Finney wrote, "To talk of inability to obey the moral law is to talk nonsense,"[6] He believed the law of God was practical and was in accord with man's nature. He preached the rightness, the wholesomeness, intelligence, practicality and reasonableness of the moral law. This exalted the Lawmaker instead of preaching the law as hard, rigid, arbitrary, burdensome, and as if it robbed man of fun or freedom. Do not the Scriptures state, "The Lord commanded us to do all these statutes, to fear the Lord our God, for our good always, that he might preserve us alive, as it is this day." (Deuteronomy 6:24; also Deuteronomy 20:12–13).

The moral law is like a fence on a farm. It not only shows ownership but provides protection. This is not to say that by keeping the moral law one will go to heaven, but it does show ownership (Romans 6:16). The moral law is treated today as if it were merely advice or as pretty fair old down-home admonition. The true Christian keeps the law, by virtue of his right relationship with God and his fellowmen, without being

[6]Charles G. Finney, *Finney's Systematic Theology*, Bethany Fellowship, Inc., Minneapolis, MN, p. 3.

aware of keeping it. The Holy Spirit will lend credence to this kind of preaching, which does not have the effect of making the Father "arbitrary," and the result will be great conviction of sin and a sense of the presence of His Spirit. "For this is the love of God, that we keep his commandments: and his Commandments are not grievous [or burdensome]" (I John 5:3).

ATONEMENT

The preaching that Jesus died as an exact literal payment for sin, rendering God merciful and forgiving, robs our God of His many lovable characteristics. Atonement is, properly, an arrangement by which the literal infliction of the penalty due to sin may be avoided; it is something which may be substituted in the place of punishment. It is that which will answer the same end secured by the literal infliction of the penalty of the law.

Atonement is not a commercial transaction—a matter of debt and payment, of profit and loss. It pertains to the law; not to literal debt and payment. Sin is crime, not debt; it is guilt, not failure in a pecuniary obligation. This is not to say that God does not have governmental problems in forgiving the unrepentant and unbelieving sinner. Nor does it mean that Jesus' death was neither vicarious nor in our spiritual place.

The only means in all the universe to subdue the rebellious heart and uphold the moral government of God is the love shown for us on Calvary. It was the greatest and most profound event of all history. The death of the Lord Jesus did not render God merciful but was an expression of His mercy. The atonement is the governmental provision for the forgiveness of sins, providing man meets the conditions of repentance and faith toward our Lord Jesus Christ. The atonement pertains to love, mercy, truth and kindness, as well as justice. It regards a race of offenders with compassion and seeks to alleviate and lessen suffering. It is not therefore the cold and stern business of paying the debt of the mere demands of justice.

It seeks to bring back wanderers by expressing God's love and forgiveness, and that salvation is free for all men if they choose to avail themselves of it. It is real, not imaginary salvation.

HUMANISTIC INVASION

Humanism has so pervaded Christianity today that very little theology and teaching has not been infected. Liberal theology cannot be sure about any life after death, but offers to make man happier during his earthly journey. On the other hand, much evangelical theology and teaching is now mainly concerned with man's happiness after he dies by holding out the joys and rewards of heaven as the main motive for Christian allegiance. In both cases, God is simply the means to the end of the individual's happiness.

While true religion will produce happiness for man, it is not the end for which we should live. Religion, a right relationship with God and our fellowmen, must be an end in itself, and not simply a means to an end.

> Now the end of the commandment is charity out of a pure heart, and of a good conscience, and of faith unfeigned (I Timothy 1:5 KJV)

VII

Conclusion

Some of the answers to the problems brought in by Trojan Horses, I have already mentioned. I am only a layman in these disciplines we have explored. Even if I had the space to deal with all the problems, and suggest solutions to the problems, I most certainly am not capable of giving all the solutions. I really have very few answers. The gospel of our Lord Jesus Christ was never intended to solve *all* the ailments of the world since it is primarily the vehicle through which the Spirit is taking out a people for his namesake. However, when it is intelligently and lovingly *applied* to any situation, the answers are forthcoming. As Christians, applying the gospel to every area of our life and our world, we would do well to remember the world doesn't care how much we know until they know how much we care. The best apologetic for Christ is still the transformed life.

Most people want a bland, flaccid, vapid, passive and sterile type of Christianity that will take them to heaven when they die but not make any stringent demands on their present lifestyle. Neither the Bible nor Christ ever taught such an insipid religion that gives hope or comfort to the passive, fearful and unbelieving (Revelation 21:7–8).

I close with the admonition of Paul. "Meditate upon these things; give thyself wholly to them; that thy profiting may appear to all. Take heed unto thyself, and unto the doctrine; continue in them: for in doing this thou shalt both save thyself, and them that hear thee." (I Timothy 4:15–16).

Appendix I

Incipiency of the Will As A Noumenal Concept

The *incipiency of the will* means that man, due to his being created in the image of God (who has creativity and a free will) also has a free will and the ability to originate his own choices.[1] The incipiency of the will means that man can and does originate his own actions or choices apart from any outside or inside influence. Man can say yes or no to a good influence and he can say yes or no to a bad influence. This phrase, incipiency of the will, was very common in textbooks of the last century.

Teaching antithetical to the incipiency of the will is found in nearly every branch of modern psychology

[1]It means that the will of a person is the origin of all his acts. The term "incipiency" indicates that the will is the commencement of all acts.

and sociology, a most flagrant example being B. F. Skinner's behaviorism.

Dr. Karl Menninger, in his book *Whatever Became of Sin,* notes:

> It seems quite clear in retrospect that the power of self-regulation has been seriously neglected in medicine.
>
> To admit the notion of any 'voluntary' control is to acknowledge that such intangibles as idealism and conscience and 'will' do play a determining role. My intention here is to resist the total translation of all 'sins' and 'crimes' into the category of symptoms. Some criminal behavior may be the result of an expression of sickness, but not all criminals are sick. Indeed, few of them are, in my experience. To admit of voluntarism is to deny the absolute positivism espoused by B. F. Skinner, who believes that even what is apparently voluntary behavior is completely determined, i.e., 'predetermined.'
>
> The disciples of Skinnerism can be just as bigoted and stubborn as the moralists and legalists who believe that everything not accidental is voluntary. The latter view makes everyone responsible for everything while the Skinnerism position discards all 'responsibility' as a myth (Its adherents are, nevertheless, forever exhorting the rest of us to voluntarily cast aside our ignorant

superstitions and voluntarily concur in their views!)[2]

Psychology, sociology, and much of our modern theology, seems to have difficulty differentiating between an influence and a causation. You can refuse to yield to an influence, but a causation cannot be resisted. Causation is a physical term, not a moral term. Most of the time when we hear the word "cause" used, it is misused, and upon further questioning we usually find that the word which should have been used was "reason." Even David Hume, the renowned atheistic philosopher, said there were uncaused causes, which has a redundant ring to it, and seems to mean that the origination of ideas or actions are sometimes not caused by anyone or anything but are accidental. Ecclesiastes 9:11 confirms that some events are accidental.

Kant tried to refute some of Hume's statements, such as "a miracle is a violation or exception to a physical law." However, this removes it from the realm of law unless you are referring to the indeterminancy principle, which doesn't apply here because it operates in the sub-atomic level and is, therefore, physical. Kant coined a word which is very important: The word is noumenon.

[2]Dr. Karl Menninger, *Whatever Became of Sin*, Hawthorn Books, Inc., pp. 78–79.

NOUMENON OR NOUMENAL

Noumenon means: 1) an object of purely intellectual intuition, as opposed to an object of sensuous perception; 2) a thing-in-itself, independent of sensuous or intellectual perception. It is the opposite of phenomenon, upon which all physical sciences are based. If science cannot verify its experiments or concepts through the senses, then there is no objective truth, as if that is the only kind of truth.[3]

A noumenal concept is above and beyond the grasp and boundaries of science. Very few people seem to be aware that science has boundaries. A noumenal concept may be defined as something that is conceived by reason and consequently thinkable, in spite of the fact that is not knowable by the five senses.

The incipiency of the will is a noumenal concept and the greatest mystery of mankind. That is why Jesus, in Mark 6:6, "marvelled at their unbelief." The word *marvel* is also used in Matthew 8:10. It means profound astonishment. Please notice Christ did not try to psychoanalyze their decision. Christ did not marvel because of His human limitations: the Scriptures record many instances of the Father's astonishment over man's illogical and nonsensical misuse of free will.

When a corporation is bought or sold there is a very important noumenal concept considered. It is called "good will." In the purchase price of a corporation, the difference between net worth and the

[3]Ninian Smart, *Philosophers and Religious Truth,* SCM Press, London WCI.

selling price is good will. Financial analysts know that "good will" is impossible to accurately evaluate and quantify.

DESCARTES ON INCIPIENCY

For Descartes, the most important ideas are innate ideas of the mind—"those," he says "that are born with me" which he perceives "clearly and distinctly" and which are like images or pictures of the reality they represent. Hence the principle implicit not only in Cartesianism, but in the whole body of modern idealism, is that all that can be known clearly and distinctly as constituting the idea of a thing may be said of the thing itself; there is no opaque residue to defeat the intellect as in the Aristotelian conception of matter and form.[4]

FREE WILL

The Bible teaches that God is not willing that any should perish, but that God's Spirit is moving upon all men to bring them to Christ. Therefore, if men are perishing, it must be because they want to perish.

What is caused cannot be free, responsible or accountable, and what is free cannot be caused or it isn't free. That which is free is accountable and responsible if it is sentient being. We are living in what should be called a Freudian day. When a person does even evil things we ask, "What caused him to do

[4]Arthur Wollaston, *Descartes' Discourse on Method,* Penguin Books, Inc., Baltimore, MD, p. 19.

that?", thereby attempting to relieve him of his responsibility.

MODERN ECONOMICS

The manner in which economics is taught is usually different than the social sciences:

> Economists begin their analysis of human behavior with the assertion that human beings act and do so with a purpose. That purpose is to improve their lots—to change the situation from something less desired to something better.
>
> This is the ultimate foundation of economics as a discipline. We only need note that people do make decisions. Such a position has several implications. First, in economics people are assumed to be "rational" in the sense that they are able to determine within limits what they want and will strive to fulfill as many of these wants as possible. People are able to offset environmental, social, and biological forces that would otherwise determine what they do. To what extent they are able to accomplish this depends on the resources at their commands and the intensity of desire to overcome these forces. Many will argue, at least for the purposes of their theories, that a factor such as the environment determines–not influences–

human behavior. The economist, on the other hand, looks at such factors as constraints within which the individual's preference can operate.

This position implies that the individual will always choose more of what he or she wants than less. It also means that he or she will choose less of what he or she does not want than more[5].

SOCIOLOGY

Much of sociology would have us believe that all of man's actions are conditioned by environment, and as we change environment, we will correspondingly see a change or improvement in man's character. While there isn't any doubt that the ghetto has great influence, it sill isn't a *cause*. The person coming from the poor, shoddy, criminal environment over which he had no choice can take heart in this: Our great God will take this into consideration. "Will not the judge of all the earth do right?"

One of the most recent developments in sociology, the attempt to administer the *coup de grace* to morality, is the teaching that three out of every ten people are born "chemically dependent," which is an excuse for alcoholism and drug addition. This attempt at

[5]McKenzie and Tullock, *The New World of Economics*, Richard D. Erwin Press, Inc., Homewood, Illinois, 1978, p. 9.

"scientific analysis" and their statistics, we can do without.

The philosophical term "seminal thinker," meaning the power of origination, is synonymous with the theological concept of the incipiency of the will, which puts the responsibility of our actions upon us, not our heredity, training or environment.[6]

The following is an admirable rebuttal of current psychological and sociological wisdom: "It is the goal of self-determined direction which motivates the child's behavior. He does not simply react to forces which impinge on him at any given moment, either from the outside world or within him. We see the individual actively interacting with his environment rather than passively responding to a given stimulus determining or causing his reactions."[7]

REVIVALS

During the course of the 17th, 18th and 19th centuries, Christians found themselves faced with some heavy questions. Before revival would come men of God would investigate issues such as:

> Does man originate his own actions . . . and is he therefore responsible for them?
>
> Is salvation man's voluntary acceptance of

[6]See Mark 1:14–15; Rev. 3:20; Matt. 13:34; Rom. 10:9–13; Luke 14:25–33 and hundreds of other passages.

[7]Rudolf Dreikurs and Loren Gray, *Logical Consequences*, Hawthorn Books, Inc., New York.

God's mercy? Or Does salvation result from God's 'election' and causation?

Throughout Christian history, it has been very commonly held that man's will is the deciding factor in salvation. Any person who realizes God never does anything arbitrarily and truly understands the word "sovereign," knows there is nothing to reconcile between the sovereignty of God and the free will of man.

Various leaders prior to and during the Reformation did not believe in the theological concept of inability.

Melancthon, a leading Lutheran theologian and writer, spoke of three causes of salvation: Scripture, the Holy Spirit and the will of man, who does not reject Scripture but accepts it.

The Arminian movement in Holland, which differed with Calvinism over the freedom of the will and the atonement, spread the idea of the freedom of the will to a considerable extent throughout Europe and America. The concept of man's free will was spread further by the Methodists, the General Baptists of England (the word "general" had reference to their view of the atonement as opposed to that of St. Anselm), the Free Will Baptists of America and the Northern and Southern Baptists. The great New England revivals of the 19th century developed "New England" or "New School" theology among Congregational and Presbyterian churches. Some of the great preachers of this persuasion were N. W. Taylor, Charles G. Finney,

Asa Mahan, Henry P. Tappan, D. D. Whedon, Albert T. Bledsoe, John Wesley, John Wesley Redford, Johnathan Goforth, Benjamin Randall and George Whitefield. Whitefield, a Calvinist, had revivals by preaching against the excesses of Calvinism and admonishing people that "They must be born again."

If we are to have revival in our day, these same truths will have to be understood, because through them the Holy Spirit convinces men they are guilty. Guilty men see their need of a Savior. To phrase it another way, men must be shown they are lost before they can be saved. The gospel is only "good news" to guilty sinners, not to *careless* sinners.

While man is pathetically guilty it would be well to remember that the individual is unique, important (so important Christ died for him) and valuable because he is made in the image of God. The severity of a penalty is the measure of the importance of the object the law protects. Man, being made in the image of God, is so valuable and important that God sent His Son to die.

Appendix II

Absolute in the Moral Sense

A major impetus behind this tendency to psychiatrize social problems arises from the vacuum of absolutes in our culture. Psychiatry has been willing to sanctify its values with the holy water of medicine and offer them up as the true faith of "Mental Health". It is a false Messiah.[1]

In a day when values clarification, social engineering and situation ethics are being taught in our grade and high schools, a few words about moral absolutes need to be written. People who teach against moral absolutes are ignorant of the design of man. All sin is a violation of our design and can have nothing but sad consequences. To teach that "thou shalt not steal ordi-

[1] E. Fuller Torrey, M.D., *The Death of Psychiatry*, Penguin Books, Inc., New York.

narily" makes as much sense as saying to a paratrooper in training, "thou shalt not jump out of an airplane at 5000 feet without a parachute ordinarily." The only real difference might be in the length of time for the consequences to take effect.

In Romans 1:29 and 30, there is a list of sins, some of which are not listed in the Ten Commandments. Nevertheless, the Bible says that people who commit these transgressions are "without understanding" and they are not natural to man (Romans 1:31).

Moral Law is a rule of moral action with sanctions (or consequences) for conformity and non-conformity. It is that rule to which moral beings ought to conform all their voluntary actions, and it is that rule which describes how they are *required* to act rather than how they *will act*. The *spirit of the law* is the reason or motive for keeping the law, the principle or purpose behind it. The ultimate spirit of the law is love, which comes from a pure heart, a good conscience and sincere faith (I Timothy 1:5). The letter of the law is its literal meaning without regard to the motive or principle behind it. This deals with the outward keeping of the law. The letter of the law may change, but the spirit behind it is immutable (absolute and unchangeable). It is possible to break the letter of the law without breaking the spirit of the law (Matthew 12:1–5, 10–13) and it is also possible to keep the letter of the law and yet break the spirit of the law. (Matthew 5:28, 6:2,5; 23:23; Romans 2:27)

True obedience to the law is not simply outward observance but comes from within, from the motive or reason behind the outward act. (Matthew 23:27–28; Romans 2:29; 7:6; II Corinthians 3:6)

When the New Testament speaks of "The Law," it is usually in reference to the expression of moral law which is absolute and unchanging, as given through the Ten Commandments. The civil and ceremonial laws as precepts of moral law ceased to be obligatory with the atonement of our Lord Jesus Christ, although the spirit of the law, or the principle of love and benevolence behind them, are immutable.

George Nash's outstanding work *The Conservative Intellectual Movement in America* takes a look at absolutes:

> "To the liberals from Samuel Adams to Harry S. Truman, there was never any room for disagreement. In the context of morals, politics and economics, liberalism was corrupt. And its corruption stemmed from one corrupting influence, the doctrine that "all absolutes are evil with the exception of the absolute state." In a system which held as relative all restraints of truth, justice, honor where could the liberal find balance or a sure foundation."[2]

Webster's *New World Dictionary* defines "absolute" as: 1) perfect; 2) complete, whole; 3) not mixed; pure; 4) actual; real; as an absolute truth.

[2]George Nash, *The Conservative Intellectual Movement in America*, Basic Books, New York, p. 103.

In the realm of moral law, I think absolute would mean the laws are real, not imagined (such as the physical law of gravity), and are not to be trifled with unless you want the penalty, punishment or consequences which are attached or inherent in the law. Accordingly, "absolution" means a formal freeing (from guilt) or forgiveness for disobeying an absolute moral law. Physical laws are rules *of* action and moral laws are rules *for* action.

David Hume said a miracle is a "violation or exception" to natural law. But if a physical law has any exceptions, it isn't a law. I think a miracle is brought about by invoking a higher physical law which at this time we do not understand, but will some day. For example, we cannot literally see God and live as we are now constituted because we don't have the necessary physical equipment, but some day when we have the incorruptible body, we will have the equipment to see God literally.

The American Heritage Dictionary of the English Language defines "absolute" as: 1) perfect in quality or nature; complete; 2) not mixed; pure, unadulterated; 3) not limited by exceptions or restrictions, unconditional; 4) not to be doubted or questioned; positive; certain. In numerical control, absolute means a fixed point of reference. In law, absolute means complete and unconditional; having no encumbrance; final. In philosophy, it means something regarded as the ultimate basis of all thoughts and beings; something regarded as independent of and unrelated to anything else.

> The absolute is a term used by philosophers to signify the ultimate reality regarded as one and yet as the source of variety; as *complete*, or *perfect*; and yet as not divorced from the finite imperfect world.[3]

The term "absolute" was introduced into the philosophical vocabulary at the very end of the eighteenth century by Schelling and Hegel and was naturalized into English by Coleridge as early as 1809–1810. The philosophers have two kinds of absolutes but as far as moral absolutes are concerned, it can be shown that Kant, Fichte, Schelling and, on occasion, Hegel, believed in moral absolutes.

The present-day practice of high school and college teachers to deny the existence of moral absolutes seems to be *almost* a 20th century phenomenon and cannot be supported by scholarship. Absolute idealism as a philosophy of the last century is not by a country mile the denial of moral absolutes.[4]

Moral relativism leads to situation ethics which really is saying, "Thou shalt not steal ordinarily." When a person is really in a right relationship with God, which implies one lives in the realm of answered prayers, he doesn't need "situation ethics." It kind of reminds us that there isn't a fine line between faith and

[3]*The Encyclopedia of Philosophy*, Collier-MacMillan. See article, "Absolute."

[4]See William James, *A Pluralistic Universe*, Macmillan in 1909, chapters 2 and 3. Also, G. E. Moore, *Some Main Problems of Philosophy*, London, 1953, chapters 8 and 9.

presumption. That line is obliterated when we use the brains God gave us to use, disciplined in His Word in obedience to His Son.

We must stress a Christianity that can deliver man from the guilt and power of sin which starts a cleansing of the motive (Titus 3:5) of the heart and leads to obedience to our Lord. Otherwise our religion will be nothing but enlightened self-interest, as Freud would accuse. Without this, evangelicalism is humanism conquering or invading Christianity.

The decline of truth-seeking in the field of contemporary psychology has left staggering consequences, namely the dissolving of moral absolutes. To make value judgments that describe "good" or "bad" behaviors is seen as unprofessional and inappropriate. Psychologists regard themselves as social scientists and not philosophers given to drawing subjective conclusions concerning what is right and what is wrong.

Even though by definition a psychiatrist is a healer of the soul, it is considered by many presumptuous and unscientific to even deal with an individual's moral problems as the root behind emotional upset. The reason for this is obvious. Man is a moral being. God has made him to think, reason, and to come to intelligent conclusions regarding what is right and proper behavior. Through His Word and through relationship with God, man knows what he ought to do to fulfill the highest good of God and his fellowman. The point is that man is responsible to God for his actions. God sets the standard. Man does not have to create his own. To say that a problem lies in an individual's behavior or wrong responses, means that one must have a standard from which to determine "wrong" behavior and an answer as to who that individual is responsible to and why. If a psychologist is to seriously consider the validity of value judgments, he must first evaluate where those judgments come from. Rather than go to the source, which is God, and have to contend with his own responsibility, it is somehow easier to try not to make "value judgments" or attribute the judgments as cultural expectations, the typical cop-out. Meanwhile, we see the statistics of how few people have been helped to overcome their emotional problems through such methods as psychoanalysis, and we marvel at the many obvious inconsistencies.

For instance, psychology is regarded as a science. Science, according to its own definition, is subject to empirical testing. In other words, one must be able to repeat a certain phenomena several times under the same circumstances and end up with the exact same conclusion each time. In its very essence, psychology and psychiatry are disciplines of the "mind" and the "soul". How does one put a "soul" in a test tube for empirical scrutinizing? How does one put a "moral mind" in a test tube to verify its existence? They are not physiological parts that can be dissected and yet it is evident that they exist. Is psychology truly a science or does it deal in the realm of mysticism? If the mind does consist of an individual's thoughts, imaginations, areas of creativity, moral standards, etc., how is one to effectively deal with disturbances within the mind or emotions apart from dealing with the above areas? Certainly within that realm, a psychologist cannot neglect the fact that his patient may be in distress because his problem is not physical. It's moral! But as long as psychology refuses to acknowledge this sense of moral behavior, and continues to view man's irresponsibility as a "disease", then we can expect to continue to see little real success in emotional healing.

The movement away from the realm of common sense and intellectual honesty is most obvious on college campuses where a student can now take classes in counseling where the professors do not believe in counseling, and classes in learning, where the educators do not believe in learning. Such nonsense can only continue with such trends of thought that disgrace the name of science and intellectual pursuit.

While an engineering or scientific absolute is a fixed point of reference, so is a moral absolute. A moral absolute is an imperative of intelligence. The Holy Scripture teaches that man has an outer and an inner revelation and this is what Immanuel Kant meant when he said, "Two matters fill me with ever-renewed wonder: the starred heaven above me and the moral law within me."[5] (Psalm 19:1; Roman 1:19, 20; 3:15; John 1:9) Absolute truth means having no restrictions, exceptions or qualifications.

Some would falsely accuse me of equating

[5]Carl J. Friederich, *The Philosophy of Kant*, The Modern Library, New York, p. xiv.

Christianity with moralism. I believe absolutism is the opposite of present day moral relativism. It should be thought of as it is taught in Axiology: the view that standards of value (moral or aesthetic) are absolute, objective, eternal and are necessary because of the nature of men and things.

Disbelief has never yet altered any facts. Were a man to deny the fact of gravity and to step out of an airplane flying high above the earth, his denial of reality would do nothing to stop him from experiencing the immediate and drastic consequences of his action. Today it is common for men and women to deny the existence of moral absolutes. But refusing to acknowledge that man has a specific design and that he is responsible to fulfill that design will result in grave consequences just as surely as stepping out of an airplane without a parachute. The consequences are certain in both instances. The only difference will be in the length of time between the occurence of the action and the reaping of the consequences. Sometimes it seems as if man would be better off if the consequences of moral choices were as immediate as the consequences of physical choices. However, our short life on this earth affords the only opportunity in eternity for man to make the choice whether to live for themselves in supreme selfishness or to live and bring glory and happiness to our Creator and happiness and well-being to our fellowman. It is the hope that more will choose the latter which motivates God to postpone some of the consequences of our moral choices for a time. Such is the mercy and love of our great God.

Appendix III

Pedagogy for Humanism

Letting these wolves call themselves humanists is like letting them wear sheep's clothing or stamping GOLD on lead bricks. They have used a very old word trick in their efforts to gain converts to their view and protect themselves from attack. Most of us were taught in history that humanism meant what Erasmus said it meant, placing the love of man above the bureaucratic and political interests of the church in Rome. Now can a Christian attack anyone who seems to come in the name of the Lord? (If you want to shout down all of your opponents, you start a free speech movement or if you want to take away people's freedoms of choice, you start a human rights movement. Certainly, people will eventually catch onto your hypocrisy, but by that time it is usually too late.) You can call them out from under their disguise using several labels.

Neohumanist simply says that they are not the same as the originals but allows them to claim some of the same virtues.

Parahumanist says they are outside the accepted traditions of humanism and (like parapsychology) may be a bit off-color.

Superhumanist could (if properly handled) be used to ridicule their aspirations to assume the role of God.

In the same vein, not all scientists (psychologists, sociologists, etc.) believe in determinism. Some do, some don't, and most have never given the matter much thought. Call the wolves out of the flock by referring to them as determinists. B. F. Skinner, Mary Calderone, Julian Huxley, Bertrand Russell, Brock Chisholm, Herman J. Muller, Elizabeth Force, Alan Guttmacher, Melvin Ketchel, Robert Harper, Wilbur J. Cohen, Paul Erlich, Erich Fromm, Margaret Mead, Lester Kirkendall, Gordon Allport, Masters and Johnson, Carl Rogers, Parul-Kurt and Hugh Hefner should be classified as superhumanists. These people represent a group of people who seem unaware that the word *cause* or *causation* is a word designating a physical action while *reason* denotes thinking or an antecedent of a moral action.

Appendix IV

Liberal Vignette

There once was a man who thought he was dead. His concerned wife and friends sent him to a doctor. The doctor decided to cure him by convincing him of one fact that contradicted his belief that he was dead. The doctor used the simple truth that dead men do not bleed. He put his patient to work reading medical texts, observing autopsies, etc. After weeks of effort, the patient finally said, "All right, all right! You have me convinced. Dead men don't bleed." Whereupon the doctor struck him in the arm with a needle, and the blood flowed. The man looked down with a contorted face and cried, "Good grief! Dead men bleed after all!"

If one holds to unproved theories with sufficient tenacity, the truth will make no difference at all, and you will be able to create a world all of your own, totally unrelated to reality and totally unable to be touched by truth. Such a condition is comparable to the man who thought he was dead. Facts made no difference, and therefore his condition was equivalent to death, because connection with the living world was severed. The man in the story not only thought he was dead, but in a very real sense he was dead. Facts no longer meant anything to him. He had committed intellectual suicide. Dead men don't think!

Appendix V

About the Author

Harry Conn, born in Lafayette, Indiana, studied mechanical engineering and related subjects at Lewis Institute of Technology, Armour Institute of Technology, Illinois Institute of Technology and Chicago University. He received an Sc.D. in Applied Science from Colorado Polytechnic. After working for John Deere Harvester Company, International Harvester, Buick and Studebaker, he was employed by La Salle Engineering of Chicago and New York. He then became Chief Engineer of Scully-Jones of Chicago from 1948 until 1961.

Mr. Conn was, until he retired in December 1977, a Group Executive of the Esterline Corporation, with responsibility for four firms reporting to him. He was also Board Chairman of the W. A. Whitney Corporation, an Esterline firm, in Rockford, Illinois.

He has written hundreds of technical articles for over 75 engineering and science journals and he contributed to the textbook *Fundamentals of Design*. In 1975 Mr. Conn received the Society of Manufacturing Engineers International Gold Medal. He has been a lecturer on engineering and lay theology in over 80 universities, colleges and seminaries in the United States, Canada, Mexico, Europe and the Orient.

Mr. Conn has twice received the Freedom Foundation's George Washington Medal and is listed in *Who's Who of Engineering, Who's Who in Business and Finance, International Businessman's Who's Who* and Marquis' new *Who's Who in the World*.

In 1975 he also received The American Society of Mechanical Engineers Edwin F. Church gold medal which stated that Conn "contributed more than anyone else to extend mechanical engineering education in manufacturing, and who had for many years devoted his talents to serve and inspire his fellow men in enriching and furthering their careers and usefulness."

Appendix VI

Humanist Manifesto I

The Manifesto is a product of many minds. It was designed to represent a developing point of view, not a new creed. The individuals whose signatures appear, would, had they been writing individual statements, have stated the proposition in differing terms. The importance of the document is that more than thirty men have come to general agreement on matters of final concern and that these men are undoubtedly representative of a large number who are forging a new philosophy out of the materials of the modern world.

It is obvious that many others might have been asked to sign the Manifesto had not the lack of time and the shortage of clerical assistance limited our ability to communicate with them. The names of several who were asked do not appear. Reasons for their absence appear elsewhere in this issue of The New Humanist. *Further criticisms that we have been unable to publish have reached us; all of them we value. We invite an expression of opinion from others. To the extent possible* The New Humanist *will publish such materials.*

Raymond B. Bragg (1933)

The time has come for widespread recognition of the radical changes in religious beliefs throughout the modern world. The time is past for mere revision of traditional attitudes. Science and economic change have disrupted the old beliefs. Religions the world over are under the necessity of coming to terms with new conditions created by a vastly increased knowledge and experience. In every field of human activity, the vital movement is now in the direction of a candid and explicit humanism. In order that religious humanism may be better understood we, the undersigned, desire to make certain affirmations which we believe the facts of our contemporary life demonstrate.

There is great danger of a final, and we believe fatal, identification of the word *religion* with doctrines and methods which have lost their significance and which are powerless to solve the problem of human living in the Twentieth Century. Religions have always been means for realizing the highest values of life. Their end has been accomplished through the interpretation of the total environing situation (theology or world view), the sense of values resulting therefrom (goal or ideal), and the technique (cult) established for realizing the satisfactory life. A change in any of these factors results in alteration of the outward forms of religion. This fact explains the changefulness of religions through the centuries. But through all changes religion itself remains constant in its quest for abiding values, an inseparable feature of human life.

Today man's larger understanding of the universe, his scientific achievements, and his deeper appreciation of brotherhood, have created a situation which requires a new statement of the means and purposes of religion. Such a vital, fearless, and frank religion capable of furnishing adequate social goals and personal satisfactions may appear to many people as a complete break with the past. While this age does owe a vast debt to traditional religions, it is nonetheless obvious that any religion that can hope to be a synthesizing and dynamic force for today must be shaped for the needs of this age. To establish such a religion is a major necessity of the present. It is a responsibility which rests upon this generation. We therefore affirm the following:

First: Religious humanists regard the universe as self-existing and not created.

Second: Humanism believes that man is a part of nature and that he has emerged as the result of a continuous process.

Third: Holding an organic view of life, humanists find

that the traditional dualism of mind and body must be rejected.

Fourth: Humanism recognizes that man's religious culture and civilization, as clearly depicted by anthropology and history, are the product of a gradual development due to his interaction with his natural environment and with his social heritage. The individual born into a particular culture is largely molded to that culture.

Fifth: Humanism asserts that the nature of the universe depicted by modern science makes unacceptable any supernatural or cosmic guarantees of human values. Obviously humanism does not deny the possibility of realities as yet undiscovered, but it does insist that the way to determine the existence and value of any and all realities is by means of intelligent inquiry and by the assessment of their relation to human needs. Religion must formulate its hopes and plans in the light of the scientific spirit and method.

Sixth: We are convinced that the time has passed for theism, deism, modernism, and the several varieties of "new thought."

Seventh: Religion consists of those actions, purposes, and experiences which are humanly significant. Nothing human is alien to the religious. It includes labor, art, science, philosophy, love, friendship, recreation—all that is in its degree expressive of intelligently satisfying human living. The distinction between the sacred and the secular can no longer be maintained.

Eighth: Religious humanism considers the complete realization of human personality to be the end of man's life and seeks its development and fulfillment in the here and now. This is the explanation of the humanist's social passion.

Ninth: In place of the old attitudes involved in worship and prayer the humanist finds his religious emotions expressed in a heightened sense of personal life and in a cooperative effort to promote social well-being.

Tenth: It follows that there will be no uniquely religious emotions and attitudes of the kind hitherto associated with belief in the supernatural.

Eleventh: Man will learn to face the crises of life in terms of his knowledge of their naturalness and probability. Reasonable and manly attitudes will be fostered by education and supported by custom. We assume that humanism will take the path of social and mental hygiene and discourage sentimental and unreal hopes and wishful thinking.

Twelfth: Believing that religion must work increasingly for joy in living, religious humanists aim to foster the creative in man and to encourage achievements that add to the satisfactions of life.

Thirteenth: Religious humanism maintains that all associations and institutions exist for the fulfillment of human life. The intelligent evaluation, transformation, control, and direction of such associations and institutions with a view to the enhancement of human life is the purpose and program of humanism. Certainly religious institutions, their ritualistic forms, ecclesiastical methods, and communal activities must be reconstituted as rapidly as experience allows, in order to function effectively in the modern world.

Fourteenth: The humanists are firmly convinced that existing acquisitive and profit-motivated society has shown itself to be inadequate and that a radical change in methods, controls, and motives must be instituted. A socialized and cooperative economic order must be established to the end that the equitable distribution of the means of life be possible. The goal of humanism is a free and universal society in which people voluntarily and intelligently cooperate for the common good. Humanists demand a shared life in a shared world.

Fifteenth and last: We assert that humanism will: (a) affirm life rather than deny it; (b) seek to elicit the possibilities of life, not flee from it; and (c) endeavor to establish the conditions of a satisfactory life for all, not merely for the few. By this positive *morale* and intention humanism will be guided, and from this perspective and alignment the techniques and efforts of humanism will flow.

So stand the theses of religious humanism. Though we consider the religious forms and ideas of our fathers no longer adequate, the quest for the good life is still the central task for mankind. Man is at last becoming aware that he alone is responsible for the realization of the world of his dreams, that he has within himself the power for its achievement. He must set intelligence and will to the task.

Humanist Manifesto I first appeared in *The New Humanist,* May/June 1933 (Vol. VI, No. 3).
Humanist Manifesto II first appeared in *The Humanist,* September/October 1973 (Vol. XXXIII, No. 5).

Signers
J. A. C. Fagginer Auer*
E. Burdette Backus*
Harry Elmer Barnes*
L. M. Birkhead*
Raymond B. Bragg*
Edwin Arthur Burtt
Ernest Caldecott*
A. J. Carlson*
John Dewey*
Albert C. Dieffenbach*
John H. Dietrich*
Bernard Fantus*
William Floyd*
F. H. Hankins*
A. Eustace Haydon*
Llewellyn Jones*
Robert Morss Lovett*
Harold P. Marley*
R. Lester Mondale*
Charles Francis Potter*
John Herman Randall, Jr.
Curtis W. Reese*
Oliver L. Reiser*
Roy Wood Sellars*
Clinton Lee Scott
Maynard Shipley*
W. Frank Swift*
V. T. Thayer
Eldred C. Vanderlaan*
Joseph Walker*
Jacob J. Weinstein
Frank S. C. Wicks*
David Rhys Williams*
Edwin H. Wilson

*Deceased

Humanist Manifesto II

Preface

It is forty years since *Humanist Manifesto I* (1933) appeared. Events since then make that earlier statement seem far too optimistic. Nazism has shown the depths of brutality of which humanity is capable. Other totalitarian regimes have suppressed human rights without ending poverty. Science has sometimes brought evil as well as good. Recent decades have shown that inhuman wars can be made in the name of peace. The beginnings of police states, even in democratic societies, widespread government espionage, and other abuses of power by military, political, and industrial elites, and the continuance of unyielding racism, all present a different and difficult social outlook. In various societies, the demands of women and minority groups for equal rights effectively challenge our generation.

As we approach the twenty-first century, however, an affirmative and hopeful vision is needed. Faith, commensurate with advancing knowledge, is also necessary. In the choice between despair and hope, humanists respond in this *Humanist Manifesto II* with a positive declaration for times of uncertainty.

As in 1933, humanists still believe that traditional theism, especially faith in the prayer-hearing God, assumed to love and care for persons, to hear and understand their prayers, and to be able to do something about them, is an unproved and outmoded faith. Salvationism, based on mere affirmation, still appears as harmful, diverting people with false hopes of heaven hereafter. Reasonable minds look to other means to survival.

Those who sign *Humanist Manifesto II* disclaim that they are setting forth a binding credo; their individual views would be stated in widely varying ways. This statement is, however, reaching for vision in a time that needs direction. It is social analysis in an effort at concensus. New statements should be developed to supersede this, but for today it is our conviction that humanism offers an alternative that can serve present-day needs and guide humankind toward the future.

Paul Kurtz, Editor, *The Humanist*

Edwin H. Wilson, Editor Emeritus,
The Humanist

The next century can be and should be the humanist century. Dramatic scientific, technological, and ever-accelerating social and political changes crowd our awareness. We have virtually conquered the planet, explored the moon, overcome the natural limits of travel and communication; we stand at the dawn of a new age, ready to move farther into space and perhaps inhabit other planets. Using technology wisely, we can control our environment, conquer poverty, markedly reduce disease, extend our lifespan, significantly modify our behavior, alter the course of human evolution and cultural development, unlock vast new powers, and provide humankind with unparalleled opportunity for achieving an abundant and meaningful life.

The future is, however, filled with dangers. In learning to apply the scientific method to nature and human life, we have opened the door to ecological damage, overpopulation, dehumanizing institutions, totalitarian repression, and nuclear and biochemical disaster. Faced with apocalyptic prophesies and doomsday scenarios, many flee in despair from reason and embrace irrational cults and theologies of withdrawal and retreat.

Traditional moral codes and new irrational cults both fail to meet the pressing needs of today and tomorrow. False "theologies of hope" and messianic ideologies, substituting new dogmas for old, cannot cope with existing world realities. They separate rather than unite peoples.

Humanity, to survive, requires bold and daring

measures. We need to extend the uses of scientific method, not renounce them, to fuse reason with compassion in order to build constructive social and moral values. Confronted by many possible futures, we must decide which to pursue. The ultimate goal should be the fulfillment of the potential for growth in each human personality—not for the favored few, but for all of human kind. Only a shared world and global measures will suffice.

A humanist outlook will tap the creativity of each human being and provide the vision and courage for us to work together. This outlook emphasizes the role human beings can play in their own spheres of action. The decades ahead call for dedicated, clear-minded men and women able to marshall the will, intelligence, and cooperative skills for shaping a desirable future. Humanism can provide the purpose and inspiration that so many seek; it can give personal meaning and significance to human life.

Many kinds of humanism exist in the contemporary world. The varieties and emphases of naturalistic humanism include "scientific," "ethical," "democratic,""religious," and "Marxist" humanism. Free thought, atheism, agnosticism, skepticism, deism, rationalism, ethical culture, and liberal religion all claim to be heir to the humanist tradition. Humanism traces its roots from ancient China, classical Greece and Rome, through the Renaissance and the Enlightenment, to the scientific revolution of the moden world. But views that merely reject theism are not equivalent to humanism. They lack commitment to the positive belief in the possibilities of human progress and to the values central to it. Many within religious groups, believing in the future of humanism, now claim humanistic credentials. Humanism is an ethical process through which we all can move, above and beyond the divisive particulars, heroic personalities, dogmatic creeds, and ritual customs of past religions or their mere negation.

We affirm a set of common principles that can serve as a basis for united action—positive principles relevant to the present human condition. They are a design for a secular society on a planetary scale.

For these reasons, we submit this new *Humanist Manifesto* for the future of humankind; for us, it is a vision of hope, a direction for satisfying survival.

RELIGION

First: In the best sense, religion may inspire dedication to the highest ethical ideals. The cultivation of moral devotion and creative imagination is an expression of genuine "spiritual" experience and aspiration.

We believe, however, that traditional dogmatic or authoritarian religions that place revelation, God, ritual, or creed above human needs and experience do a disservice to the human species. Any account of nature should pass the tests of scientific evidence; in our judgment, the dogmas and myths of traditional religions do not do so. Even at this late date in history, certain elementary facts based upon the critical use of scientific reason have to be restated. We find insufficient evidence for belief in the existence of a supernatural; it is either meaningless or irrelevant to the question of the survival and fulfillment of the human race. As nontheists, we begin with humans not God, nature not deity. Nature may indeed be broader and deeper than we now know; any new discoveries, however, will but enlarge our knowledge of the natural.

Some humanists believe we should reinterpret traditional religions and reinvest them with meanings appropriate to the current situation. Such redefinitions, however, often perpetuate old dependencies and escapisms; they easily become obscurantist, impeding the free use of the intellect. We need, instead, radically new human purposes and goals.

We appreciate the need to preserve the best ethical teachings in the religious traditions of humankind, many of which we share in common. But we reject those features of traditional religious morality that deny humans a full appreciation of their own potentialities and responsibilities. Traditional religions often offer solace to humans, but, as often, they inhibit humans from helping themselves or experiencing their full potentialities. Such institutions, creeds, and rituals often impede the will to serve others. Too often traditional faiths encourage dependence rather than independence, obedience rather than affirmation, fear rather than courage. More recently they have generated concerned social action, with many signs of relevance appearing in the wake of the "God is Dead" theologies. But we can discover no divine purpose or providence for the human species. While there is much that we do not know, humans are responsible for what we are or will become. No deity will save us; we must save ourselves.

Second: Promises of immortal salvation or fear of eternal damnation are both illusory and harmful. They distract humans from present concerns, from self actualization, and from rectifying social injustices. Modern science discredits such historic concepts as the "ghost in the machine" and the "separable soul". Rather, science affirms that the human species is an emergence from natural evolutionary forces. As far as we know, the total personality is a function of the biological organism transacting in a social and cultural context. There is no credible evidence that life survives the death of the body. We continue to exist in our progeny and in the way that our lives have influenced others in our culture.

Traditional religions are surely not the only obstacles to human progress. Other ideologies also impede human advance. Some forms of political doctrine, for instance, function religiously, reflecting the worst features of orthodoxy and authoritarianism, especially when they sacrifice individuals on the altar of utopian promises. Purely economic and political viewpoints, whether capitalist or communist, often function as religious and ideological dogma. Although humans undoubtedly need economic and political goals, they also need creative values by which to live.

ETHICS

Third: We affirm that moral values derive their source from human experience. Ethics are *autonomous* and *situational*, needing no theological or ideological sanction. Ethics stem from human need and interest. To deny this distorts the whole basis of life. Human life has meaning because we create and develop our futures. Happiness and the creative realization of human needs and desires, individually and in shared enjoyment, are continuous themes of humanism. We strive for the good life, here and now. The goal is to pursue life's enrichment despite debasing forces of vulgarization, commercialization, bureaucratization, and dehumanization.

Fourth: Reason and intelligence are the most effective instruments that humankind possesses. There is no substitute: neither faith nor passion suffices in itself. The controlled used of scientific methods, which have transformed the natural and social sciences since the Renaissance, must be extended further in the solution of human problems. But reason must be tempered by humility, since no group has a monopoly of wisdom or virtue. Nor is there any guarantee that all problems can be solved or all questions answered. Yet critical intelligence, infused by a sense of human caring, is the best method that humanity has for resolving problems. Reason should be balanced with compassion and empathy and the whole person fulfilled. Thus, we are not advocating the use of scientific intelligence independent of or in opposition to emotion, for we believe in the cultivation of feeling and love. As science pushes back the boundary of the known, man's sense of wonder is continually renewed, and art, poetry, and music find their places, along with religion and ethics.

THE INDIVIDUAL

Fifth: The preciousness and dignity of the individual person is a central humanist value. Individuals should be encouraged to realize their own creative talents and desires. We reject all religious, ideological, or moral codes that denigrate the individual, suppress freedom, dull intellect, dehumanize personality. We believe in maximum individual autonomy consonant with social responsibility. Although science can account for the causes of behavior, the possibilities of individual *freedom of choice* exist in human life and should be increased.

Sixth: In the area of sexuality, we believe that intolerant attitudes, often cultivated by orthodox religions and puritanical cultures, unduly repress sexual conduct. The right to birth control, abortion, and divorce should be recognized. While we do not approve of exploitive, denigrating forms of sexual expression, neither do we wish to prohibit, by law or social sanction, sexual behavior between consenting adults. The many varieties of sexual exploration should not in themselves be considered "evil." Without countenancing mindless permissiveness or unbridled promiscuity, a civilized society should be a *tolerant* one. Short of harming others or compelling them to do likewise, individuals should be permitted to express their sexual proclivities and pursue their lifestyles as they desire. We wish to cultivate the development of a responsible attitude toward sexuality, in which humans are not exploited as sexual objects, and in which intimacy, sensitivity, respect, and honesty in interpersonal relations are encouraged. Moral education for children and adults is an important way of developing awareness and sexual maturity.

DEMOCRATIC SOCIETY

Seventh: To enhance freedom and dignity the individual must experience a full range of *civil liberties* in all societies. This includes freedom of speech and the press, political democracy, the legal right of opposition to governmental policies, fair judicial process, religious liberty, freedom of association, and artistic, scientific, and cultural freedom. It also includes a recognition of an individual's right to die with dignity, euthanasia, and the right to suicide. We oppose the increasing invasion of privacy, by whatever means, in both totalitarian and democratic societies. We would safeguard, extend and implement the principles of human freedom evolved from the *Magna Carta* to the *Rights of Man*, and the *Universal Declaration of Human Rights*.

Eighth: We are committed to an open and democratic society. We must extend *participation democracy* in its true sense to the economy, the school, the family, the workplace, and voluntary associations. Decision-making must be decentralized to include widespread involvement of people at all levels—social, political, and economic. All persons should have a voice in developing the values and goals that determine their lives. Institutions should be responsive to expressed desires and needs. The conditions of work, education, devotion, and play should be humanized. Alienating forces should be modified or eradicated and bureaucratic structures should be held to a minimum. People are more important than decalogues, rules, proscriptions, or regulations.

Ninth: The separation of church and state and the separation of ideology and state are imperatives. The state should encourage maximum freedom for different moral, political, religious, and social values in society. It should not favor any particular religious bodies through the use of public monies, nor espouse a single ideology and function thereby as an instrument of propaganda or oppression, particularly against dissenters.

Tenth: Human societies should evaluate economic systems not by rhetoric or ideology, but by whether or not they *increase economic well-being* for all individuals and groups, minimize poverty and hardship, increase the sum of human satisfaction, and enhance the quality of life. Hence the door is open to alternative economic systems. We need to democratize the economy and judge it by its responsiveness to human needs, testing results in terms of the common good.

Eleventh: The principle of moral equality must be furthered through elimination of all discrimination based upon race, religion, sex, age, or national origin. This means equality of opportunity and recognition of talent and merit. Individuals should be encouraged to contribute to their own betterment. If unable, then society should provide means to satisfy their basic economic, health, and cultural needs, including, wherever resources make possible, a minimum guaranteed annual income. We are concerned for the welfare of the aged, the infirm, the disadvantaged, and also for the outcasts—the mentally retarded, abandoned or abused children, the handicapped, prisoners, addicts—for *all* who are neglected or ignored by society. Practicing humanists should make it their vocation to humanize personal relations.

We believe in the *right to universal education*. Everyone has a right to the cultural opportunity to fulfill his or her unique capacities and talents. The schools should foster satisfying and productive living. They should be open at all levels to any and all; the achievement of excellence should be encouraged. Innovative and experimental forms of education are to be welcomed. The energy and idealism of the young deserve to be appreciated and channeled to constructive purposes.

We deplore racial, religious, ethnic, or class antagonisms. Although we believe in cultural diversity and encourage racial and ethnic pride, we reject separations which promote alienation and set people and groups against each other; we envision an *integrated* community where people have a maximum opportunity for free and voluntary associaiton.

We are *critical of sexism or sexual chauvinism* — male or female. We believe in equal rights for both women and men to fulfill their unique careers and potentialities as they see fit, free of invidious discrimination.

WORLD COMMUNITY

Twelfth: We deplore the division of humankind on nationalistic grounds. We have reached a turning point in human history where the best option is to *transcend the limits of national sovereignty* and to move toward the building of a world community in which all sectors of the human family can participate. Thus we look to the development of a system of world law and a world order based upon transnational federal government. This would appreciate cultural pluralism and diversity. It would not exclude pride in national origins and accomplishments nor the handling of regional problems on a regional basis. Human progress, however, can no longer be achieved by focusing on one section of the world, Western or Eastern, developed or underdeveloped. For the first time in human history, no part of humankind can be isolated from any other. Each person's future is in some way linked to all.

Thus we reaffirm a commitment to the building of world community, at the same time recognizing that this commits us to some hard choices.

Thirteenth: This world community must *renounce the resort to violence and force* as a method of solving international disputes. We believe in the peaceful adjudication of differences by international courts and by the development of the arts of negotiation and compromise. War is obsolete. So is the use of nuclear, biological, and chemical weapons. It is a planetary imperative to reduce the level of military expenditures and turn these savings to peaceful and people oriented uses.

Fourteenth: The world community must engage in *cooperative planning* concerning the use of rapidly depleting resources. The planet Earth must be considered a single *ecosystem*. Ecological damage, resource depletion, and excessive population growth must be checked by international concord. The cultivation and conservation of nature is a moral value; we should perceive ourselves as integral to the sources of our being in nature. We must free our world from needless pollution and waste, responsibly guarding and creating wealth, both natural and human. Exploitation of natural resources, uncurbed by social conscience, must end.

Fifteenth: The problems of *economic growth and development* can no longer be resolved by one nation alone; they are worldwide in scope. It is the moral obligation of the developed nations to provide—through an international authority that safeguards human rights—massive technical, agricultural, medical, and economic assistance, including birth-control techniques, to the developing portions of the globe. World poverty must cease. Hence extreme disproportions in wealth, income, and economic growth should be reduced on a worldwide basis.

Sixteenth: Technology is a vital key to human progress and development. We deplore any necromantic efforts to condemn indiscriminately all technology and science or to counsel retreat from its further extension and use for the good of humankind. We would resist any moves to censor basic scientific research on moral, political, or social grounds. Technology must, however, be carefully judged by the consequences of its use; harmful and destructive changes should be avoided. We are particularly disturbed when technology and bureaucracy control, manipulate, or modify human beings without their consent. Technological feasibility does not imply social or cultural desirability.

Seventeenth: We must expand communication and transportation across frontiers. Travel restriction must cease. The world must be open to diverse political, ideological, and moral viewpoints and evolve a worldwide system of television and radio for information and education. We thus call for full international cooperation in culture, science, the arts, and technology *across ideological borders*. We must learn to live openly together or we shall perish together.

HUMANITY AS A WHOLE

In closing: The world cannot wait for a reconciliation of competing political or economic systems to solve its problems. These are the times for men and women of good will to further the building of a peaceful and prosperous world. We urge that parochial loyalties and inflexible moral and religious ideologies be transcended. We urge recognition of the common humanity of all people. We further urge the use of reason and compassion to produce the kind of world we want—a world in which peace, prosperity, freedom, and happiness are widely shared. Let us not abandon that vision in despair or cowardice. We are responsible for what we are or will be. Let us work together for a humane world by means commensurate with humane ends. Destructive ideological differences among communism, capitalism, socialism, conservatism, liberalism, and radicalism should be overcome. Let us call for an end to terror and hatred. We will survive and prosper only in a world of shared humane values. We can initiate new directions for humankind: ancient rivalries can be superseded by broad-based cooperative efforts. The commitment to tolerance, understanding, and peaceful negotiation does not necessitate acquiescence to the status quo nor the damming up of dynamic and revolutionary forces. The true revolution is occurring and can continue in countless nonviolent adjustments. But this entails the willingness to step forward onto new and expanding plateaus. At the present juncture of history, commitment to all humankind is the highest commitment of which we are capable; it transcends the narrow allegiances of church, state, party, class, or race in moving toward a wider vision of human potentiality. What more daring a goal for humankind than for each person to become, in ideal as well as practice, a citizen of a world community. It is a classical vision; we can now give it new vitality. Humanism thus interpreted is a moral force that has time on its side. We belive that humankind has the potential intelligence, good will, and cooperative skill to implement this commitment in the decades ahead.

We, the undersigned, while not necessarily endorsing every detail of the above, pledge our general support to *Humanist Manifesto II* for the future of humankind. These affirmations are not a final credo or dogma but an expression of a living and growing faith. We invite others in all lands to join us in further developing and working for these goals.

Lionel Abel, professor of English, State University of New York at Buffalo
Khoren Arisian, board of leaders, New York Society for Ethical Culture
Isaac Asimov, author
George Axtelle, professor emeritus, Southern Illinois University
Archie J. Bahn, professor of philosophy emeritus, Univ. of New Mexico
Paul H. Beattie, president, Fellowship of Religious Humanists

Malcolm Bissell, professor emeritus, University of Southern California
H. J. Blackham, chairman, Social Morality Council, Great Britain
Brand Blanshard, professor emeritus, Yale University
Paul Blanshard, author
Joseph L. Blau, professor of religion, Columbia University
Sir Hermann Bondi, professor of mathematics, King's College, University of London
Howard Box, leader, Brooklyn Society for Ethical Culture
Raymond B. Bragg, minister emeritus, Unitarian Chapter, Kansas City
Theodore Brameld, visiting professor, C.U.N.Y.
Brigid Brophy, author, Great Britain
Lester R. Brown, Senior Fellow, Overseas Development Council
Bette Chambers, president, American Humanist Association
John Ciardi, poet
Francis Crick, M.D., Great Britain
Arthur Danto, professor of philosophy, Columbia University
Lucien de Coninck, professor, University fo Gand, Belgium
Miriam Allen de Ford, author
Edd Doarr, Americans United for Separation of Church and State
Peter Draper, M.D., Guy's Hospital Medical School, London
Paul Edwards, professor of philosophy, Brooklyn College
Albert Ellis, executive director, Institute of Advanced Study Rational Psychotherapy
Edward L. Ericson, board of leaders, New York Society for Ethical Culture
H. J. Eysenck, professor of psychology, University of London
Roy P. Fairfield, coordinator, Union Graduate School
Herbert Feigl, professor emeritus, University of Minnesota
Raymond Firth, professor emeritus of anthropology, University of London
Anthony Flew, professor of philosophy, the University, Reading, England
Kenneth Furness, exec. secretary, British Humanist Association
Erwin Gaede, minister, Unitarian Church, Ann Arbor, Michigan
Richard S. Gilbert, minister, First Unitarian Church, Rochester
Charles Wesley Grady, minister, Unitarian Universalist Church, Arlington, Virginia
Maxine Green, professor, Teachers College, Columbia University
Thomas C. Greening, editor, Journal of Humanistic Psychology
Alan F. Guttmacher, president, Planned Parenthood Federation of America

J. Harold Hadley, minister, Unitarian Church, Pt. Washington, N.Y.
Hector Hawton, editor, Question, Great Britain
A. Eustace Haydon, professor emeritus of history of religions
James Hemming, psychologist, Great Britain
Palmer A. Hitty, administrative secretary, Fellowship of Religious Humanists
Hudson Hoagland, president emeritus, Worcester Fundation for Experimental Biology
Robert S. Hoagland, editor, Religious Humanism
Sidney Hook, professor emeritus of philosophy, New York University
James F. Hornback, leader, Ethical Society of St. Louis
Irving Louis Horowitz, editor, Society
James M. Hutchinson, minister emeritus, First Unitarian Church, Cincinnati
Mordecai M. Kaplan, rabbi, founder of Jewish Reconstruction Movement
John Kidneigh, professor of Social Work, University of Minnesota
Lester A. Kirkendall, professor emeritus, Oregon State University
Margaret Knight, University of Aberdeen, Scotland
Jean Kotkin, executive secretary, American Ethical Union
Richard Kostelanetz, poet
Paul Kurtz, editor, The Humanist
Lawrence Lader, chairman, National Association for Repeal of Abortion Laws
Edward Lamb, president, Lamb Communications, Inc.
Corliss Lamont, chairman, National Emergency Civil Liberties Union
Chauncey D. Leake, professor, University of California, San Francisco
Alfred McClung Lee, professor emeritus, sociology-anthropology, C.U.N.Y.
Elizabeth Briant Lee, author
Christopher Macy, director, Rationalist Press Association, Great Britain
Clorinda Margolis, Jefferson Community Mental Health Center, Philadelphia, Pennsylvania
Joseph Margolis, professor of philosophy, Temple University
Harold P. Marley, retired, Unitarian minister
Floyd W. Matson, professor of American Studies, University of Hawaii

Vashti McCollum, former president, American Humanist Association
Lloyd Morain, president, Illinois Gas Co.
Mary Morain, editorial board, International Society for General Semantics
Henry Morgentaler, M.D., past president, Humanist Association of Canada
Charles Morris, professor emeritus, University of Florida
Mary Mothersill, professor of philosophy, Barnard College
Jerome Nathanson, chairman of the board of leaders, New York Society of Ethical Culture
Billy Joe Nichols, minister, Richardson Unitarian Church, Texas
Kai Nielsen, professor of philosophy, University of Calgary, Canada
P. H. Howell-Smith, professor of philosophy, York University, Canada
Chaim Perglman, professor of philosophy, University of Brussels, Belgium
James W. Prescott, National Institute of Child Health and Human Development
Harold J. Quigley, leader, Ethical Humanist Society of Chicago
Howard Radest, professor of philosophy, Ramapo College
John Herman Randall, Jr., professor emeritus, Columbia University
Oliver L. Reiser, professor emeritus, University oif Pittsburgh
Robert G. Risk, president, Leadville Corp.
Lord Ritchie-Calder, formerly University of Edinburgh, Scotland
B. T. Rocca, Jr., consultant, International Trade and Commodities
Andre D. Sakharov, Academy of Sciences, Moscow, U.S.S.R.
Sidney H. Scheuer, professor emeritus, Claremont Graduate School
Clinton Lee Scott, Universalist minister, St. Petersburg, Florida
Roy Woods Sellars, professor emeritus, University of Michigan
A. B. Shah, president, Indian Secular Society
B. F. Skinner, professor of psychology, Harvard University
Kenneth J. Smith, leader, Philadelphia Ethical Culture schools
A. Solomon, coordinator, India Secular Society, Bombay
Matthew les Spetter, chairman, department ethics, Ethical Culture Schools
Mark Starr, chairman, Eperanto Information Center
V. M. Tarkunder, president, All India Radical Humanist Association, New Delhi
Harold Taylor, project director, World University Student Project
V. T. Taylor, author

Herbert A. Tonne, education board, Journal of Business Education
Jack Tourin, president, American Ethical Union
E. C. Vanderland, lecturer
J. P. van Praag, chairman, International Humanist and Ethical Union, Utrecht
Maurice B. Visscher, M.D. professor emeritus, University of Minnesota
Goodwin Watson, association coordinator, Union Graduate School
Gerald Wendt, author
Henry N. Wieman, professor emeritus, University of Chicago
Edwin H. Wilson, executive director emeritus, American Humanist Association
Georgia H. Wilson, retired, Political Science Department, Brooklyn College
H. Van Rensselaer Wilson, retired, Political Science Department, Brooklyn College
Sherman Wine, rabbi, Society for Humanist Judaism
Bertram D. Wolfe, Hoover Institution
Alexander S. Yesenin Volpin, mathematician
Marvin Zimmer, professor of philosophy, State University of New York at Buffalo

The above list is only a partial one, other signatures are being added. Institutions are listed for identification only.

Recommended Further Reading:

If you enjoyed this book, we suggest that you order one or more of the following titles from your local Christian bookstore or from the publisher: ***Mott Media, Inc., 1000 East Huron Street, Milford, Michigan, 48042.***

Are Textbooks Harming Your Children?, by James Hefley. Shocking exposé of material discovered in public school textbooks. Paper, **$4.95**

The Creator in the Courtroom: Scopes II, by Norman Geisler. Documentation and evaluation of what really occurred at the 1981 Arkansas Creation-Evolution trial. Paper, **$5.95**

Fundamentals for American Christians, by Russ Walton. Basic biblical principles of government which Christians in the U.S. should understand. Paper, **$5.95**

The God They Never Knew: The Tragedy of Religion Without Relationship, by George Otis, Jr. The author stresses that the naked essence of Christianity is a personal love relationship. A linking of theology to living and experiencing the Christian life. Paper, **$5.95**

How to Make the Right Decisions, by John Arnold and Bert Thompkins. Shows the reader not only how to evaluate problems sensibly, but how to make the *right* decisions in a Christian, moral and ethical way. Paper, **$5.95**

Management for the Christian Leader, by Olan Hendrix. This book clearly and thoroughly explores the major issues of management in a positive, organized and comprehensive course for every Christian in a position of leadership. Cloth, **$8.95**

Picking Up the Pieces: Successful Single Living for the Formerly Married, by Clyde Besson. This book repairs shattered dreams, enlightens, inspires, and helps people cope with the trauma of a dissolved marriage. Paper, **$5.95**

The Reconstruction of the Republic, by Harold O. J. Brown. A thought-provoking book on the problems that face America. America desperately needs a reconstruction—and this brilliant, boldly forthright book outlines a blueprint. Paper, **$5.95**

The Scripture of Truth: A Layman's Guide to Understanding How the Bible Is Inspired, by George and Charlotte Syme. This book brings together for the benefit of all interested laymen all phases of the doctrine of Scripture. A clear, comprehensive and comprehensible study on how we got our Bible, how we know it is authoritative and how we know we can trust it. Paper, **$5.95**

Secular Humanism: Man Striving to Be God, essays by Ern Baxter, Howard Carter, Robert Grant, R. J. Rushdoony and Bob Sutton. Humanism is clearly not only a religion but the summation of all antichristianity. Paper, **$2.95**

The Separation Illusion, by John Whitehead. A lawyer examines the First Amendment and refutes the idea that there is a wall of separation between our religious beliefs and our civil government. Paper, **$5.95**

Social Justice and the Christian Church, by Ronald Nash. Arguing from his stance as a theological and political conservative, Nash subjects the recent trend toward the support of socialism to careful scrutiny. His book seeks to expose the specious character of this trend to the Bible as well as to expose its faulty analysis of economics. Cloth, **$12.95**

Student Survival Manual, by Randy Rodden. A pocket gem of inspirational reading, designed for all students of the Bible. Rodden builds a powerful defense of the Bible's authenticity, and refutes the skeptics who question it. Paper, **$2.95**

What Would Jesus Do Now?, by Wes Neal. A serious look at how to become Christ-like. A practical approach on how to follow Jesus Christ more closely in our routine, daily living situation. Paper, **$5.95**

Who Am I and What Am I Doing Here?, by Mark W. Lee. Lee brings the Christian discussion to its rightful place in the current exchange of ideas about personal identity. Cloth, **$9.95**; Paper, **$5.95**

The Wisdom of God, by David Jeremiah. A search into the Scripture for the meaning of the wisdom of God and how to know God's wisdom in our life. Provides simple how-to's for God's people. Paper, **$5.95**